D0930182

THE WORLD WAR II D-DAY INVASION IN AMERICAN HISTORY

R. Conrad Stein

Enslow Publishers, Inc.

40 Industrial Road   PO Box 38
Box 398   Aldershot
Berkeley Heights, NJ 07922   Hants GU12 6BP
USA   UK

http://www.enslow.com

Library of Congress Cataloging-in-Publication Data

Stein, R. Conrad.
   The World War II D-Day invasion in American history / R. Conrad
Stein.
      p. cm. — (In American history)
   Summary: Discusses the events surrounding the D-Day invasion of
Europe by Allied Forces on June 6, 1944.
   Includes bibliographical references and index.
   ISBN 0-7660-2136-X
   1. World War, 1939-1945—Campaigns—France—Normandy—
Juvenile literature. [1. World War, 1939-1945—Campaigns—France—
Normandy.] I. Title: World War Two D-Day invasion in American
history. II. Title: World War 2 D-Day invasion in American history.
III. Title. IV. Series.
   D756.5.N6S74   2003
   940.54'2142—dc21

                                        2003008141

Printed in the United States of America

10 9 8 7 6 5 4 3 2 1

To Our Readers: We have done our best to make sure all Internet Addresses in
this book were active and appropriate when we went to press. However, the
author and the publisher have no control over and assume no liability for the
material available on those Internet sites or on other Web sites they may link to.
Any comments or suggestions can be sent by e-mail to comments@enslow.com or
to the address on the back cover.

Illustration Credits: Enslow Publishers, Inc., pp. 26, 30, 53, 96;
National Archives and Records Administration, pp. 4, 8, 12, 13, 17, 18,
21, 23, 25, 34, 42, 48, 55, 57, 68, 74, 77, 82, 88, 92, 97, 99, 100;
R. Conrad Stein, pp. 62, 70, 101.

Cover Illustration: National Archives and Records Administration

★ Contents ★

American paratroopers, inside their aircraft, wait to take off just before D-Day.

THE FIRST STRIKE

On the night of June 5, 1944, more than twelve hundred transport aircraft waited on airfields in southern England. Most were C-47 Dakota airplanes, which held up to twenty American paratroopers. The airborne troops inside the planes were packed in shoulder-to-shoulder. Still, many of the men sat alone with their thoughts: Will I die on the soil of France? Will I lose an arm, or a leg, or suffer some other ghastly wound? Will the Germans use poison gas? The Americans were young and superbly trained, but only a few had seen actual combat. Doubts and fears ran wild through their minds on this tense night during World War II.

One by one, the planes rumbled skyward and climbed into the darkness. Moving in tight formations, almost wingtip to wingtip, this huge fleet of aircraft headed over the English Channel. The paratroopers were supposed to jump out of the planes, float to the earth on their parachutes, and begin the great D-Day invasion.

Flying in one Dakota was Lieutenant Robert Mathias. He was a platoon leader in the American

82nd Airborne Division. At age twenty-eight, Mathias was one of the oldest of the D-Day paratroopers. An excellent boxer and a devout Catholic, Mathias was a tough but fair officer. He was also a father figure to the young troopers. During the two-hour flight across the Channel, Mathias often grinned at his men to give them an added spark of confidence.

Over the coast of France, the enemy unleashed a furious storm of anti-aircraft fire. It looked like the world's grandest fireworks display—orange tracer bullets streaming through the night, shells bursting everywhere. But this was not the Fourth of July and the men were not sitting on park benches in their hometowns. This was war. Enemy gunners were trying desperately to kill them.

As the plane approached its assigned target zone Lieutenant Mathias shouted, "Stand up and hook up."[1] Obeying their leader, the men rose and clipped their parachute release straps to the wire (called the static line) running along the plane's ceiling. Mathias stood at the open door waiting for the green light above to flick on. That green light would indicate that the aircraft was over its proper area (the drop zone). Mathias would then lead the men on their jump. Outside, shell bursts from antiaircraft guns shook the Dakota.

Almost at the same time the green light lit up, a shell fragment smashed into Mathias's chest, knocking him backward. Somehow, Mathias climbed to his feet, raised his arm to signal his men to follow, and jumped into the night. The lieutenant's body was found half an hour later. It is possible he died before his feet even hit the ground. Lieutenant Robert Mathias was the first American officer to be killed on D-Day.

D-Day, the long-awaited invasion of France, was a bold gamble. Even if successful, it could have cost thousands of lives. It was also the most complex operation ever attempted in any war. It involved five thousand ships and eleven thousand aircraft. More than one hundred seventy-five thousand men and fifty thousand vehicles were to land on beaches on the first day alone. Invading troops came from the United States, Great Britain, Canada, Australia, New Zealand, Poland, and France. In all, twelve nations cooperated in the military endeavor. Roughly three-quarters of the men participating were American. On D-Day these nations rose up together to strike a deadly blow against an enemy many people regarded as evil.

Newly homeless children sit amid the wreckage of their London neighborhood after a German bombing raid in September 1940.

*F*ate demands from us no more than from the great men of German history. As long as I live I shall think only of the victory of my people. I shall shrink from nothing and I shall anni-hilate everyone who is opposed to me . . . I want to annihilate the enemy![1]

—Adolf Hitler, speaking to his generals at the start of World War II.

CONQUERED EUROPE

By D-Day, World War II had already been raging for almost five years. Never before had the world seen such a destructive conflict. When it finally ended in September 1945, World War II had taken an estimated 55 million lives.

Blitzkrieg

Many historians agree that World War II was caused by a host of problems left unresolved from World War I. Germany was the major defeated power in World War I, which was fought in Europe from 1914 to 1918. The war left the German people dispirited and impov-erished. The victorious nations, led by Great Britain and France, imposed the harsh Treaty of Versailles on the defeated Germans. Terms of the treaty required

Germany to transfer goods such as railroad cars, ships, and even cattle to the victors. Germany also lost territory.

From the depths of German despair rose a new leader, Adolf Hitler, who took power in 1933. Hitler blamed the Communists and the Jews for Germany's postwar difficulties. According to Hitler, the Communists, who believed in government ownership of factories and farms, were poised to take over Germany. Hitler claimed the Jews controlled Germany's wealth and corrupted its government. He gained popularity in office by building highways and launching other public projects. These construction programs put unemployed Germans back to work. Most ominous for the rest of the world, Hitler rebuilt his nation's military. He ordered factories to produce tanks and ships even though the Treaty of Versailles prohibited German rearmament.

On September 1, 1939, German troops attacked Poland. France and Great Britain, Poland's allies, quickly declared war. The new conflict was called World War II. At first Germany amazed military experts with a brand of warfare called *blitzkrieg*, meaning lightning war. Masses of tanks led the way to smash into Polish territory. The tanks were followed by troops riding on trucks and armored vehicles. Protecting the tank-led columns were waves of aircraft. Staggered by the enemy's fast-moving armies, Polish forces collapsed in a little more than three weeks.

Other countries fell to the German blitzkrieg forces—Norway, Denmark, the Netherlands, and

Belgium. In May 1940, Hitler launched an all-out offensive on France. Once more, powerful tank-led troops crushed their opposition. In late May, French and British soldiers were surrounded at the French city of Dunkirk on the English Channel. By calling upon every ship able to float, the British navy managed to evacuate 336,000 soldiers from the shores of France. Four years later, the retreat from Dunkirk played on the minds of the D-Day invaders.

France officially surrendered to Germany on June 22, 1940. Hitler's mighty army had pushed its enemies into the sea. Germans were now the masters of Western Europe. A confident Adolf Hitler believed his foes would never again return to the European continent. Germany, it seemed, was invincible.

Then, soon after the fall of France, the German armed forces began to suffer reversals. Just across the narrow English Channel stood Great Britain. In the summer of 1940, Britain was Germany's last remaining foe in its push through Europe. Hitler launched an air offensive designed to weaken British defenses and allow his armies to invade English soil. However, the British people endured German bombers. In what was called the Battle of Britain, the British Royal Air Force inflicted severe losses on German aircraft. Ultimately, Hitler had to cancel his plans to cross the Channel and conquer Great Britain.

In June 1941, Hitler took his biggest gamble when he attacked the vast Soviet Union. (Russia was once part of the Soviet Union, which collapsed in 1991.)

Here the Germans practiced blitzkrieg on its largest scale. An invading force of 3 million men advanced along a battle line two thousand miles wide. Supporting the German advance were more than three thousand tanks and two thousand aircraft. In the opening

Adolf Hitler (center) poses in Paris on June 23, 1940, just after the French surrendered to the Germans.

German infantrymen (one throwing a hand grenade) advance into the Soviet Union in 1941.

months, German armored divisions raced into the heart of the Soviet Union. But the invaders were turned back at the capital city of Moscow after a bitter winter campaign. Setbacks at Moscow and over the skies of England proved to the world that the German military machine was strong but not invincible.

America Enters the War

In the United States, most people opposed Hitler. Still, public sentiment was against taking any active part in the European conflict. Many Americans embraced a policy called isolationism. According to the isolationists, the United States should stay out of overseas conflicts. Isolationists argued that the war in Europe was being fought thousands of miles from American shores. The American nation was protected from that war by the huge Atlantic Ocean. Ironically, war came to the United States from the Pacific.

Since the late 1930s, Japan had been fighting an undeclared war against China. The American government favored China in this conflict, and refused to sell Japan vital war-making material such as steel, oil, and rubber. Japanese leaders hoped to strike back at America by destroying its Pacific Fleet in one overwhelming blow. On a peaceful Sunday morning— December 7, 1941—Japanese aircraft roared over the skies of Pearl Harbor, Hawaii, dropping a deadly rain of bombs. The surprise attack killed more than two thousand Americans and shattered eighteen U.S. Navy ships. The attack on Pearl Harbor shocked and outraged Americans. Isolationism disappeared almost overnight. On December 8, the United States declared war on Japan.

Three days after the Pearl Harbor raid, Germany declared war on the United States. Historians still debate why Adolf Hitler chose to add such a powerful foe to his already large list of enemies. According to a treaty the Germans had with the Japanese, Germany did not have to ally itself with Japan in war unless a country had attacked Japan. The United States had not attacked Japan. America had the world's most advanced industries. American factories were capable of producing tanks, ships, airplanes, and other war goods in astonishing quantities. Whatever Hitler's reasons, the entry of the United States into the European war led to Germany's doom.

The Second Front

The Allies consisted of the United States, Britain, the Soviet Union, and many other nations. However, the responsibility of invading German territory from the west fell mostly on the United States and Britain. How were the Americans and the British to wage offensive warfare against the German army occupying Europe? America's top general, George C. Marshall, wanted to build up forces in the British Isles and launch a cross-channel invasion as early as 1943. This would open up a second front. Such a second front would compel the Germans to fight soldiers of the Soviet Union to their east and the Americans and British to their west. Marshall's desire to force Germany into a two-front war was shared by General Dwight D. Eisenhower, the American commander in Europe.

Opposing a 1943 cross-channel invasion was British Prime Minister Winston Churchill. The British leader argued that the Allies were not ready for such an ambitious operation. To bolster his arguments, Churchill pointed to a disastrous raid the British and Canadians had attempted on the port city of Dieppe, France, in August 1942. At Dieppe, the invaders had faced German forces far stronger than their leaders had anticipated. Of the six thousand men assaulting

Dieppe, more than three thousand were killed, wounded, or captured.

Churchill urged the British and the Americans to advance on Germany through the Mediterranean Sea to the enemy's south. The prime minister called this region Europe's "soft underbelly."

Churchill's view prevailed over the U.S. generals. The Allies assaulted North Africa in November 1942. Much of North Africa was occupied by German and Italian troops. Italy at the time was allied with Germany and, along with Japan and a few other countries, made up what was called the Axis powers. In July 1943, the Allies invaded Sicily and drove the Axis forces off that island. Then in September, the Allies landed on the shores of Italy. Each of these invasions was commanded by General Eisenhower. The American general gained valuable experience in sea-to-land operations. However, the Allied offense became bogged down in the mountainous terrain of Italy. The Mediterranean proved to be not a "soft underbelly" as Churchill predicted. Instead, the campaign in Italy was a difficult, frustrating operation.

Since 1941, the Soviet Union had been fighting a bitter and cruel war against the Germans. The war raged entirely on Soviet soil. Hundreds of battles had taken the lives of millions of soldiers and civilians. Worse yet, the Soviet people believed they were fighting virtually alone. British and American leaders feared the Soviet Union would make a separate peace with

General Dwight D. Eisenhower was the commander of Allied forces at D-Day.

Germany. This would leave the Western Allies to fight alone against Hitler.

In November 1943, Roosevelt and Churchill met with the Soviet leader Josef Stalin at Teheran, Iran. The three men assembled to discuss future war plans. Roosevelt assured the Soviet chief that plans were in place to begin a massive invasion of France in the spring of 1944. The operation, Roosevelt added, had a code name—Overlord. On the last day of the Teheran conference, Roosevelt informed Stalin that General Dwight D. Eisenhower would command the Overlord forces. Stalin seemed pleased to know that the second front in Western Europe would soon be a reality.

The "Big Three" met late in the World War II years to discuss plans for the defeat of Germany. From left to right are Prime Minister Winston Churchill of Great Britain, President Franklin D. Roosevelt of the United States, and Premier Josef Stalin of the Soviet Union.

3

OPERATION OVERLORD

You will enter the Continent of Europe and, in conjunction with the other United Nations, undertake operations aimed at the heart of Germany and the destruction of her armed forces.[1]

—A directive issued to invading troops in 1944 by the Combined Chiefs of Staff of the United States and Great Britain.

In 1942, German military men faced a dilemma— a choice between equally bad alternatives. The generals knew the Allies would soon cross the English Channel and strike continental Europe. But where? Should the German army try to defend the entire French coastline? Or should Germany concentrate its forces on the more likely invasion points?

The Atlantic Wall

Western Europe's Atlantic coast spreads three thousand miles from Holland to the French border with Spain. It would seem impossible for any nation to guard such a long seashore. Yet Adolf Hitler insisted that every inch of the coastline must be fortified. The German leader ordered army engineers to build what was called the Atlantic Wall. He envisioned a string of fifteen thousand concrete forts protected by land mines and barbed wire. This string of fortifications was to be manned by an army of three hundred thousand soldiers. It would be suicidal, Hitler felt, for any enemy to try to assault these strong coastal positions.

But how could Germany build and defend the Atlantic Wall? The nation's resources were already stretched to the breaking point. By late 1943, almost 3 million Germans were fighting in the Soviet Union and a sizable force battled the Americans and the British in Italy. German factories strained to make tanks and artillery shells to supply troops in the field. Nevertheless, Hitler demanded that the wall be built. He had fought in the trenches of World War I and had supreme confidence in the value of bunkers and fortifications.

Abiding by Hitler's orders, thousands of workers began pouring concrete and digging trenches to create the Atlantic Wall. Many were slave workers from captive nations. The workers were forced at gunpoint to build the wall and thus protect the German empire. The wall became the biggest construction job attempted by any side in World War II. It also consumed Germany's precious resources. Soon it was impossible for German industries to get concrete for other projects because it was all being poured into the Atlantic Wall. Steel, too, became scarce. Millions of steel rods were used to reinforce the Atlantic Wall's bunkers. Still, by the spring of 1944, the line of

This German bunker (an artillery emplacement) is typical of those built for the Atlantic Wall. It had concrete walls thirteen feet thick and was bombed in 1944.

fortresses Hitler desired was woefully incomplete. The wall boasted fearsomely strong emplacements in some areas. Yet, miles and miles of the coastline were virtually undefended.

Adolf Hitler and most German leaders believed the major Allied force would invade at the Pas-de-Calais, France. At the Pas-de-Calais, the narrowest point of the English Channel, only twenty miles separated the shores of England and France. A landing at the Pas-de-Calais would also put the invaders closer to major port cities and provide a shorter route to the heartland of Germany. Hence, the coast near the French city of

Calais was the most highly fortified section of the Atlantic Wall. Here stood steel fences designed to stop landing craft and tanks. Near Calais were heavy guns hidden in concrete domed bunkers ten feet thick. Allied leaders shuddered when they thought of the defenses waiting for them at Calais.

Commanding the German forces in Western Europe was sixty-nine-year-old Field Marshal Gerd von Rundstedt. He had a fine military mind. But younger officers considered him unfriendly and even arrogant. Von Rundstedt believed that the Atlantic Wall was a waste of money and manpower. He wanted trucks and tanks to form a mobile army to be held at the ready far inland. When the Allies struck the coast, these mobile forces would rush forward to drive them back to the sea. Critics reminded the field marshal that the Allies controlled the skies. Allied planes would destroy tanks and trucks while they were still on the roads. Von Rundstedt dismissed these objections. He believed the army could move at night and still reach the invasion beaches.

Holding a different view was Field Marshal Erwin Rommel, who was second in command to Von Rundstedt. Rommel had fought the Allies in the North African desert. He was such a crafty opponent that the British in Africa nicknamed him the Desert Fox. The German general was painfully aware of Allied airpower. Therefore, he thought the Atlantic Wall was Germany's best hope. He once walked along a French beach with an aide named Hellmuth Lang and said,

"The war will be won or lost on the beaches. . . . Believe me, Lang, the first twenty-four hours of the invasion will be decisive . . . for the Allies as well as Germany, it will be the longest day."[2]

Complicating the differences between Von Rundstedt and Rommel was a third commander—Adolf Hitler. The head of the German state thought himself a military genius. He spent hours poring over maps trying to determine where the Allies were likely to strike. Building the Atlantic Wall was his obsession. Hitler wanted the wall to be backed by a mobile tank force, but he demanded that only he have final say as

Field Marshal Erwin Rommel (left, wearing binoculars) was second in command of German forces defending France against an Allied invasion.

SOURCE DOCUMENT

THE STRENGTH OF THE DEFENCES WAS ABSURDLY OVERRATED. THE "ATLANTIC WALL" WAS AN ILLUSION, CONJURED UP BY PROPAGANDA— TO DECEIVE THE GERMAN PEOPLE AS WELL AS THE ALLIES. IT USED TO MAKE ME ANGRY TO READ STORIES ABOUT ITS IMPREGNABLE [UNBEATABLE] DEFENCES. IT WAS NONSENSE TO DESCRIBE IT AS A "WALL." HITLER HIMSELF NEVER CAME TO VISIT IT, AND SEE WHAT IT REALLY WAS.[3]

Field Marshal Gerd von Rundstedt's scorn for the Atlantic Wall can be seen in this interview he gave to British writer Basil Liddell-Hart after the war.

to how the bulk of the tanks were to be deployed. This split in command between Von Rundstedt, Rommel, and finally Hitler would prove fatal for the German defenders on D-Day.

Target Normandy

The Allies had no such command problem. Dwight Eisenhower was the supreme commander. Second in importance was British General Bernard Law Montgomery, whose forces had defeated Rommel's in North Africa. Many American officers thought Montgomery overly ambitious. But "Monty," as the London newspapers called him, was well respected by the British public. Eisenhower was careful to treat Monty with the utmost respect. Above all, Eisenhower was a gifted diplomat who labored to keep British and American relations in harmony.

Also aiding the Allies was the simple fact the Germans had no idea where the landings would take place. As long as the Germans were guessing, they had no choice but to employ forces along the entire coast of France. In fact, the German high command kept thousands of troops at highly unlikely invasion targets such as Norway and Holland. Clearly, the German army occupied more territory than it could properly defend. All they could do was suppose where the Allies would land. Therefore, the Germans had to spread their forces thin and try to defend every possible beach and port city.

General Bernard Montgomery was the highest British officer of the D-Day troops. Here, he is pictured in North Africa in November 1942.

As early as the summer of 1943, the Americans and the British agreed that Normandy was the best place to attempt the landing. It was hoped that a strike there would catch the Germans by surprise. In addition, the Normandy region had broad, sandy beaches that would allow landing craft to discharge troops.

Naturally, the Allies wanted to keep the Germans in doubt as to their landing spot. Allied leaders set up an elaborate spy network, called Operation Fortitude, which was designed to cast the message that the main attack would be directed at the Pas-de-Calais region.

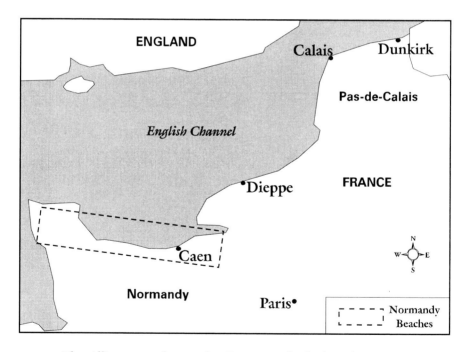

The Allies wanted to make Germany think that they were going to invade near the city of Calais. The fact that Calais was the closest point to England on the French coast further helped the Allies deceive Germany.

Operation Fortitude agents in neutral countries such as Spain entered stores and very loudly asked for prewar roadmaps near the city of Calais in France. The agents in the Spanish stores hoped that German spies would observe them as they bought the maps. Bogus radio reports from the British Isles told of a million-man army massing on the English coast opposite of Pas-de-Calais. American General George Patton, who the Germans believed would lead the invasion, visited the region frequently. Finally, the Allies made life-sized models of tanks, trucks, and landing craft and placed them along the shore facing the French city of Calais. The models were fashioned from rubber and papier-mâché. Many of the models were built by stagehands who worked in London's theater district.

Preparations

The term D-Day was first used in World War I to denote the day of an attack. The words H-Hour referred to the precise time when an offense would begin. In truth, there were many D-Days in World War II. But over the years the June 6, 1944, invasion of Normandy has assumed such historic importance that it alone emerged as the Second World War's special D-Day, overshadowing all others.

By early 1944, more than 2 million American soldiers had crossed the Atlantic and were on English soil. The Americans were joined by one million combat-ready British and Canadian troops. Countless tanks, artillery pieces, and trucks were parked end to end on farmers' fields. Some four hundred fifty thousand tons of ammunition were stuffed into storehouses. So many military goods had been stockpiled in Great Britain that a joke circulated among the troops: "If they put any more equipment on this island, it'll sink." However, the soldiers knew the coming invasion would be no joke. Also stored in Great Britain were 124,000 hospital beds. No one wanted to even think about the number of coffins that were stacked in British warehouses.

While waiting for the order to invade, the soldiers engaged in intensive training exercises. A trooper named Gordon Jones remembered, "We used to run and march eight miles to [the port city of] Erlin, get into landing craft and go out in the bay, then run down these ramps, charge ashore, back on the boats, day after day."[4] The Allies were receiving offensive training, which had an emphasis on advancing. Across the Channel, German soldiers served as laborers, building fortifications in the Atlantic Wall. Combat training for German troops consisted of defensive measures that featured men firing weapons from within their bunkers.

Soldiers preparing to invade sensed that they were about to make history. Some had little education, but still believed that they would soon participate in a military operation that people would read about for centuries to come. The majority of the men were eager to go, despite the dangers they would face. In the case of one prominent Englishman, a burning desire to be part of the invasion forces almost upset the plans.

Weeks before D-Day, British Prime Minister Winston Churchill spoke to Eisenhower and told him that he wanted to land on the beaches along with the men. "I argued," Eisenhower later wrote, "that the chance of his becoming an accidental casualty was too important from the standpoint of the whole war effort and I refused his request."[5] Churchill then said that if he could not land with the soldiers he would serve as an ordinary deckhand on one of the many ships gathering for the invasion. Eisenhower was at a loss, not knowing how to deal with the prime minister's stubbornness. Then George VI, king of England, intervened. The king told the prime minister that if he signed on as a deckhand then he—the king—would also join a ship's company and risk his life during the invasion. Churchill withdrew his request, and the argument was settled between the prime minister and the D-Day commander.

The Word To Go

Allied plans called for the invaders to land over a thirty-mile front that was divided into five beachheads. The beachheads were the prime landing areas. American soldiers would assault beachheads code-named Omaha and Utah while the British would storm Gold and Sword Beaches, and the Canadians Juno Beach. Paratroopers were to drop behind the beaches on the evening before D-Day. The airborne soldiers

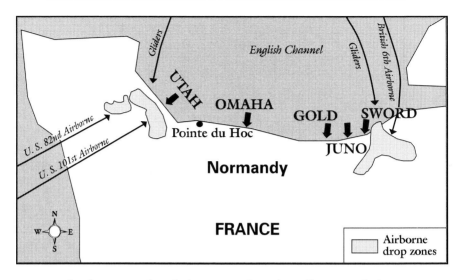

The five main beach locations that the Allies invaded on D-Day were located on the Normandy coastline beneath towering cliffs.

would prevent German reinforcements from moving toward the invasion shores. Before the landing, the Normandy coast would be pounded by bombers from the air and shelled by the big guns on naval ships.

Eisenhower wanted to start the invasion in early May 1944, but there were not enough landing craft on hand. Especially vital were the Higgins boats, which carried troops from ship to shore. Officially, they were called LCVPs (Landing Craft, Vehicle, Personnel). But most Americans called the landing craft Higgins boats, after the New Orleans company where they were made. Eisenhower later said of Andrew Higgins, who owned the company, "He is the man who won the war for us."[6] Higgins boats carried up to thirty-six fully equipped soldiers. They brought the soldiers up to the shoreline, their ramps dropped, and the men charged off. The boats then returned to a ship to pick up more infantry. During sea-to-land invasions, a few dozen troop-carrying Higgins boats were as important as a mighty battleship.

Throughout May 1944, shipments of Higgins boats and other landing craft arrived in Great Britain. In the closing days of May, everyone knew D-Day was imminent. An American sergeant named Henry Giles recorded in his diary, "The whole outfit now has a very bad case of the invasion shakes. Very little talk about anything but the assault landings, what it will be like, what the casualties will be etc. Any way you look at it, it's not going to be a piece of cake."[7]

Tides and the moon were vital factors in determining the date and time for the invasion. Twice a day the tides rose and fell over the landing beaches. A low tide exposed the concrete blocks, steel rails, and other obstacles placed on the beaches by the Germans. At high tide, those obstacles were hidden by water and could easily rip the bottoms out of landing craft. The landings had to take place when the tide was low. Moonlight was also a prime factor. The paratroopers needed at least a half-moon to provide visibility when they jumped out of their aircraft before dawn of D-Day.

The tide and the moon were favorable on June 5, the day Eisenhower chose to strike. By June 3, ships were loaded and the anxious wait began as some two hundred thousand soldiers and sailors stood by to hear orders from one man—Dwight Eisenhower. The orders never came. Rain fell in sheets and a blanket of thick clouds covered the beaches, making accurate bombing impossible. Huge waves rocked the English Channel. Eisenhower decided to postpone the invasion for one day and hope for better weather.

Near midnight on June 4, Eisenhower met with his staff. The most important staff member present was a twenty-eight-year-old British captain named J. M. Stagg. He was a meteorologist (a weather expert). Stagg told the assembly he believed the storm would ease on June 6 for at least twenty-four hours. He could not promise fair weather beyond that period, but June 6 should be calm.

Eisenhower asked the opinion of the others. British General Montgomery made no doubt about his view, "I would say—Go!"[8] The final decision was Eisenhower's alone. If he were to postpone the invasion again, he would have to wait at least two more weeks for favorable conditions of tides and the moon. Troops were at that moment on ships, tossing around in the waters of the Channel, most of them miserably seasick. Many of the men at this point had been briefed as to the Normandy landing site. If those soldiers were brought back to shore, it would be impossible to keep the invasion details secret from German spies. Eisenhower simply said, "I'm quite positive we must give the order. I don't like it, but there it is. . . . I don't see how we can possibly do anything else."[9]

The decision was made and the meeting between the highest-ranking officers in the Allied army broke up. Outside a heavy rain pelted the windows. Dwight Eisenhower drove through the storm to the house trailer he used as his quarters. The general hoped to catch a few hours of sleep before the big event. Eisenhower had just issued what many historians now regard as the most important single order of World War II. D-Day, the largest invasion ever attempted in world history, would take place on June 6, 1944.

General Eisenhower talks to American paratroopers in England, just before their D-Day jump on targets in the Normandy region.

ASSAULT FROM THE AIR

Small private wars erupted to [my] right and left. . . . The only thing I could be sure of was that a lot of men were dying in this nightmarish labyrinth.[1]

—Donald Burgett of the U. S. 101st Airborne Division describing the scene minutes after he parachuted to the ground on D-Day evening.

On the night of June 5, a young German private named Helmut Römer stood guard at the bridge over the Caen Canal near Bénouville, France. In the distance, he heard the bursting shells of antiaircraft fire. This was not uncommon in the skies above Normandy. In recent weeks, the Allies had increased their bombing raids over all of occupied France. A few of Römer's friends suggested the bombers were softening up defenses in preparation for an invasion. However, most German defenders believed their enemy would not be so foolish as to attack out-of-the-way Normandy. In fact, the average soldier thought that being stationed in Normandy was the safest duty imaginable for a German infantryman in 1944.

Suddenly, in the moonlit night, Römer saw what

looked like an airplane approach him at treetop height. But it could not be an airplane because it made no engine noise. The strange aircraft hit the ground with a screeching crash and skidded to a stop. For a few seconds all was silent. At once Römer realized the aircraft was a glider, and it was no doubt packed with paratroopers. Römer shouted out to alert his company. His warning came too late. Machine-gun fire resounded in the night, and hand grenades exploded. A battle raged that lasted only fifteen minutes. Römer managed to escape, but he knew the bridge he was assigned to guard had been captured by the enemy. The young German was also painfully aware that his safe duty on Normandy had come to a very sudden end.[2]

The bold conquest of the Caen Canal Bridge took place just after midnight on June 6. The bridge was taken by glider troops of the British 6th Airborne Division. It was the first battle of D-Day, and the engagement was a remarkable success for the Allies. Other battles waged by airborne troops in the early morning hours of June 6, 1944, had mixed success and often very bloody results.

Death and Chaos

Over the night skies above Normandy came waves of planes bearing paratroopers: 13,400 of the airborne troops were Americans and nearly 7,000 were British. The planes flew in V-shaped formations like flocks of migrating geese. Leading the formations were aircraft-carrying pathfinders. The pathfinders were specially trained troops who were slated to jump first. Once on the ground, the pathfinders were to mark drop zones with radio transmitters and flashing lights. Subsequent waves of paratroopers would then jump into those designated drop zones. The details of this airborne operation had been worked out months earlier.

The defenses the paratroopers met were a mirror of what the seagoing forces encountered just hours later. Some formations of aircraft encountered murderous antiaircraft fire, while others flew unscathed. Combat soldiers always marvel at the random nature of death during battle. Men are killed and others are spared based only on what seemed to be luck—good or bad luck.

Certainly unlucky were leading planes of the American 101st Airborne. As soon as they were over French soil, explosions rocked the aircraft, and tracer bullets lit up the night. Private Dwayne Burns saw nearby aircraft catch fire or explode. "My plane was bouncing like something gone wild," Burns later wrote. "I could hear the machine-gun rounds walking [hitting in a series] across the wings. It was hard to stand up and troopers were falling down and getting up; some were throwing up. Of all the training we had, there was not anything that had prepared us for this."[3]

Pilots swerved or climbed into the skies to escape the wall of antiaircraft fire. The violent twists and turns caused the pilots to lose their bearings. Many pathfinders dropped into the wrong zone, throwing the men behind them into mass confusion. From plane after plane, the troopers leapt into the night and landed far from their intended areas. Carefully made plans vanished in the chaotic skies over Normandy. Some airborne soldiers landed in marshes created by Rommel's engineers, who flooded inland regions to discourage parachute attack. Overloaded by equipment weighing up to one hundred pounds, men drowned in less than two feet of water. At least one plane dropped sixteen to eighteen men directly in the waters of the English Channel, where they sank like stones.

About thirty men from the 82nd Airborne found themselves floating into the center of the town of Ste.-Mère-Église. Their true drop zone was a field a few miles west. Instead they fell into the town square, where several buildings were burning, and the place was alive with Germans. Troopers drifting helplessly downward heard the town's church bell ringing an alarm. For some, the bell was the last sound they would ever hear.

PFC Ernest Blanchard landed in a tree near the center of Ste.-Mère-Église. (PFC stands for "private first class.") He struggled to free himself from his parachute while machine guns and the screams of wounded men filled the darkness all around him. In desperation, Blanchard drew his knife and hacked at his harness. Finally, he fell from the tree. Minutes later, Blanchard looked at his hand and discovered that he had cut off his thumb while trying to free himself from his own parachute. He was so panic-stricken that he had not even felt the pain of the amputation.[4]

Private John Steele's parachute was caught in the town's church steeple, leaving him dangling over the square. He was a forced witness to the slaughter below. Steele watched one man drop directly into a burning building and be consumed by the flames. Another American literally exploded in midair as bullets detonated the ammunition he carried. Steele hung from the steeple playing dead for two hours until he was finally rescued by fellow paratroopers. His plight above the town square was later dramatized in the 1962 movie *The Longest Day*.

SOURCE DOCUMENT

ALL AROUND US, THE PARATROOPERS WERE LANDING WITH A HEAVY THUD ON THE GROUND. BY THE LIGHT OF THE FIRE, WE CLEARLY SAW A MAN MANIPULATING THE CABLES OF HIS PARACHUTE [TO AVOID LANDING IN A BURNING BUILDING]. ANOTHER, LESS SKILLFUL, CAME DOWN IN THE MIDDLE OF THE FLAMES. SPARKS FLEW AND THE FIRE BURNED BRIGHTER. THE LEGS OF ANOTHER PARATROOPER CONTRACTED VIOLENTLY AS THEY WERE HIT [BY GERMAN GUNFIRE]. HIS RAISED ARMS CAME DOWN. THE GIANT PARACHUTE, BILLOWING IN THE WIND, ROLLED OVER THE FIELD WITH THE INERT BODY.[5]

The mayor of Ste.-Mère-Église, Alexandre Reynaud, was in the town square and got a ground view of the American paratroopers battling with the Germans.

Upon landing in the countryside, each man tore off his parachute and darted his head left and right looking for the enemy or—better yet—one of his buddies. Jumps were so scattered that troopers hit the ground and found no one at all. Donald Burgett of the U.S. 101st Airborne Division was one of those lost and alone: "I had no success finding anyone, friend or foe. To be crawling up and down . . . alone, deep in enemy country with a whole ocean between yourself and the nearest allies sure makes a man feel about as lonely as a man can get."[6]

American gliders landed shortly after the main body of paratroopers. The gliders were motorless aircraft that were towed by a wire behind a transport plane. Once over enemy lines, the gliders were released. They then floated downward and skidded to a landing on their bellies. Gliders carried heavier equipment—Jeeps, antitank guns, light trucks, medical supplies, and additional troops. As was true with the paratroopers, more than half the gliders came down in the wrong area. The 82nd Division's glider forces suffered 157 killed and wounded on the first night alone, a casualty rate of 16 percent. Some gliders were torn apart by "Rommel's Asparagus," poles deliberately placed in fields to serve as antiglider obstacles. Gliders also crashed into hedgerows—the fencelike earthen banks, topped with hedges, that Normandy farmers build to separate their fields.

Regrouping

Despite the general confusion, some paratroopers landed exactly where they were supposed to be. One of those was Major General Matthew Ridgeway, commander of the 82nd Airborne Division. Ridgeway came down at his appointed target in a Normandy pear tree orchard. Seconds after landing, he saw something moving in the dark and drew his pistol. "As I knelt, still fumbling in the grass," Ridgeway later wrote, "I recognized in the dim moonlight the bulky outline of a cow. I could have kissed her."[7] The presence of cows in the field meant that there were no mines there.

General Maxwell Taylor, who commanded the 101st Airborne Division, landed alone and far from where he was supposed to be. He wandered for half an hour until he discovered a young private as lost as he was. At a military base, the two would have stiffly saluted each other. Here, in a combat zone in the middle of the night, the general and the private hugged as if they were brothers. Soon General Taylor encountered two of his high-ranking officers. They bent low and studied a map with the aid of a flashlight. The three men, all of whom were expert map-readers, came to three different conclusions as to where they were.

Planners of the airborne operation expected confusion, so they issued the men a recognition device called a cricket. This was a simple snapping toy, the same item that was found in boxes of Cracker Jack. When encountering a stranger in the dim light, a trooper was

Bodies of dead paratroopers are wrapped in parachutes shortly after the D-Day assault.

to click once. If the stranger was a fellow trooper, he was to click back twice. The system worked to a degree, but there were foul-ups. A private named Len Griffing landed in a crowded area where, "There was so many clicks and counter clicks that night that nobody could tell who was clicking at whom."[8]

Almost three-quarters of the D-Day paratroopers were lost when they first touched ground. Still, after their initial bewilderment, they gathered in small groups and tried to accomplish their missions. The makeshift groups contained men from different companies and even different divisions. These were troopers who had never worked together before.

Lieutenant Jack Tallerday led a dozen or more paratroopers from the 101st and the 82nd Airborne divisions down a country road. He saw a band of eight or ten men coming toward him. Tallerday gave the one click signal and thought he heard the two return clicks. "As our two groups approached each other," Tallerday said, "it was quite evident by the configuration of their steel helmets that they were Germans."[9] But, in an oddity of battle, the two clusters of soldiers passed each other without incident. Not one man pointed his rifle at another. Not one man looked another in the eye. Though they were mortal enemies, both groups went their separate ways like strangers passing on a city street.

Winning the Night

The airborne units had specific instructions—towns to occupy, bridges to secure, roadblocks to set up. With so many men scattered far from their intended locations, the fulfillment of primary missions often became impossible. So the paratroopers exercised their secondary roles. They had been instructed that, if lost, they should at least disrupt German communications. This they did with devastating effect. Troopers cut telephone and telegraph wires and blew down telephone posts with grenades. German units, with their telephone networks knocked out, were unable to tell

---

SOURCE DOCUMENT

THE GERMANS WERE ALL AROUND US, OF COURSE, SOMETIMES WITHIN FIVE HUNDRED YARDS OF MY CP (COMMAND POST), BUT IN THE FIERCE AND CONFUSED FIGHTING THAT WAS GOING ON ALL ABOUT, THEY DID NOT LAUNCH THE STRONG ATTACK THAT COULD HAVE WIPED OUT OUR EGGSHELL PERIMETER DEFENSE. THIS WAS IN A LARGE PART DUE TO THE DISPERSION OF THE PARATROOPERS. WHEREVER THEY LANDED THEY BEGAN TO CUT EVERY COMMUNICATION LINE THEY COULD FIND, AND SOON THE GERMAN COMMANDERS HAD NO MORE CONTACT WITH THEIR UNITS THAN WE HAD WITH OURS.[10]

General Matthew Ridgway, commander of the U.S. 82nd Airborne Division, credited the disruption of phone lines with saving the paratroopers from a ruinous German counterattack. About the first night of D-Day, Ridgway wrote the above account.

other units that enemy paratroopers had landed at Normandy.

The Allies further confounded the Germans by dropping life-sized paratroop dummies over the Normandy region. Hundreds of these dummies, which were made like department store mannequins, floated downward looking for all the world like a major airborne assault. Near the French city of Le Havre, a German regiment of two thousand men spent the early morning of June 6 frantically searching the marshlands for enemy airborne soldiers. The regiment found only dummies. Of course, while the Germans were busy rooting out the dummies, they could not engage the Allied invaders.

The opening hours of the air drop appeared to be a calamity. Sixty percent of the equipment was destroyed, most radios were out of order, and a sizable number of troops were lost. Nevertheless, the airborne operation was a success. The men of the 101st and the 82nd Airborne divisions were ordered to hold the rear areas and prevent the Germans from rushing reinforcements to the invasion beaches. The paratroopers accomplished this mission despite their disorganized landings.

Ste.-Mère-Église, scene of the gory battle in the square, fell to the paratroopers in two hours. Three major roads met at Ste.-Mère-Église. The Germans needed the town in order to advance their troops toward the shore. For the next forty-eight hours, German artillery shelled Ste.-Mère-Église, but the enemy could not break the paratroopers' grip on the crossroads village. The Germans used their feared 88-millimeter gun, a highly accurate and deadly artillery piece. One paratrooper, Private John Fitzgerald, wrote:

> The ground trembled and my eardrums felt as if they would burst. Dirt was filling my shirt and was getting into my eyes and mouth. Those 88s became a legend. It was said that there were more soldiers converted to Christianity by the 88 than by Peter and Paul combined.[11]

The paratroopers were young, brash, and all were volunteers. Many eighteen- and nineteen-year-old paratroopers entered the D-Day battle seeking military glory and dreaming about winning a chest full of medals for heroism. At their first taste of bloody fighting, their illusions melted away. War, they discovered, meant agony, death, and mind-numbing fear. Still, individuals accomplished heroic feats. One such hero was Staff Sergeant Harrison Summers from West Virginia.

Summers found himself leading a group of fifteen paratroopers, all of whom were from outfits other than his own. Without bothering to learn their names, he ordered the men to take a group of stone farmhouses from German defenders. The men, fearful and insecure about taking commands from this sergeant they had never seen before, refused to move. So Summers raced to the first farmhouse alone, while the others watched from a safe distance. With his submachine gun blazing, Summers kicked in the door of the farmhouse, killed four Germans, and sent the others fleeing into the woods. He then sprinted to another house and fired upon it. Gradually, the men of Summers's quickly-assembled group began to follow this bold sergeant. In minutes, Summers and his followers cleared a row of farmhouses and drove away scores of German defenders. At the last house, Summers fell, exhausted and breathless. The staff sergeant from West Virginia was later awarded the Distinguished Service Cross, a high medal for heroism during combat.[12]

Historians who study D-Day today marvel at the actions of the paratroopers. They jumped into blinding darkness, landed on confusing terrain, and often had to fight for their lives seconds after their feet touched ground. Yet they took the Germans by surprise and defeated some of the enemy's best soldiers. D-Day might very well have failed had it not been for the valor of the Allied airborne troops.

A Catholic chaplain holds services in England for soldiers about to hit the D-Day beaches.

ASSAULT FROM THE SEA

. . . the water [below me] was just full of boats, like bunches of ants crawling around down there. I imagined all those young men huddled in the landing craft, doubtless scared to death. I could see what they were heading into and I prayed for all those brave young men. I thought, man, I'm up here looking down at this stuff and they're out there waiting to get on that beach.[1]

—Lt. A. H. Corry, a bombardier on a B-26 medium bomber flying over the landing beaches at dawn on D-Day.

German Major Werner Pluskat was worried. He was in command of an artillery unit consisting of twenty guns, which covered a broad Normandy beach. Pluskat did not know that his beach was a prime Allied target code-named Omaha. All night, hundreds of aircraft droned above Pluskat's bunker. An officer telephoned Pluskat claiming Allied paratroopers had landed to his rear. Then came other confusing reports: The parachutists were from an Allied bomber that had been shot down by antiaircraft fire; or, the parachutists were dummies.

Endlessly Pluskat peered through binoculars toward the sea. The weather was fairly calm now, but just hours earlier the English Channel had boiled with waves and was swept by fierce winds. German troops stationed in Normandy and along other parts of the Atlantic Wall usually relaxed when storms churned the Channel. The Germans reasoned the Allies would not invade in bad weather. Once more Pluskat gazed at the Channel waters with his binoculars. The dawn was beginning to break. In the dim light, the German officer saw nothing but empty sea.

Bombardment

Just beyond Pluskat's vision, the largest armada ever assembled in world history moved silently toward the coast. Counting landing craft, more than five thousand vessels bobbed in the choppy waters. Lieutenant Ray Zuker, flying in a B-24 bomber nicknamed Lady Lightning, looked down on this awesome array of ships and said, " . . . literally you could have walked, [ship to ship] if you took big steps, from one side of the Channel to the other. There were that many ships out there."[2]

Shortly after 5:00 A.M., hundreds of warships opened fire on the Normandy beaches. Sailors on the decks pressed their hands over their ears as the gunblasts rocked their ships. A veteran newspaperman named Holdbrook Bradley wrote, "The sound of battle

SOURCE DOCUMENT

As far as you could see in every direction, the ocean was infested with ships. There must have been every type of oceangoing vessel in the world. I even thought I saw a paddle-wheel steamer in the distance, but that was probably an illusion.

There were battleships and all other kinds of warships clear down to patrol boats. There were great fleets of Liberty ships. There were fleets of luxury liners turned into troop transports, and fleets of big landing craft and tank carriers and tankers. And in and out through it all were nondescript ships—converted yachts, riverboats, tugs, and barges.[3]

Riding on a ship in the invasion fleet was Ernie Pyle, America's most widely read war correspondent. Pyle had covered the war for various newspapers since its beginning. However, he had never seen a fleet the size of the one approaching the Normandy beaches.

is something I'm used to. But this [the opening bombardment on D-Day] was the loudest thing I have ever heard. There was more firepower than I've ever heard in my life."[4]

On the bluff overlooking Omaha Beach, German Major Pluskat thought his bunker was being torn apart. With each exploding shell, powdered cement fell like snow from the bunker's thick ceiling. Roars outside sounded like thunder from hell. In between shell bursts, Pluskat looked at the Channel and saw ships spreading before him like stars on a clear night. He spoke on the telephone to a disbelieving officer who was stationed miles to the rear. The officer asked where exactly the shells were falling. "For God's sake, they're falling all over," shouted Pluskat. "What do you want me to do—go out and measure the holes with a ruler?"[5]

As the ships pounded the beaches, great waves of Allied aircraft flew over Normandy. More than three thousand heavy bombers, fifteen hundred medium bombers, and fifty-four hundred fighters filled the air the first day. Only a handful of German fighter aircraft were there to resist them. Germany once had a mighty air force. But by 1944, the German air force had been pushed back to bases in Germany where the planes defended their homeland from fleets of Allied bombers. On June 6, American and British planes had the skies over Normandy pretty much to themselves.

With few fighter aircraft to harass them, Allied bombers dropped a deadly rain of bombs on enemy positions. A German machine gunner named Franz Gockel wrote:

> The bombers were suddenly over us. . . . I dove under [my] gun as bombs screamed and hissed into the sand and earth. Two heavy bombs fell on our position, and we held our breath as more explosions fell into the hinterland. Debris and clouds of smoke enveloped us; the earth shook; eyes and nose were filled with dirt, and sand ground between teeth. There was no hope for help. No German aircraft appeared, and this sector had no antiaircraft guns.[6]

Some German soldiers who lived through the bombardment from air and sea were left temporarily frozen with fear. Some defenders later suffered from a condition called shell shock, which is currently also known as post-traumatic stress disorder. This caused them to become extremely depressed or anxious; have frequent, terrifying nightmares; and have flashbacks to the horrific events they experienced. Grimly, the machine gunner Franz Gockel looked beyond the beaches at the galaxy of ships. No German shore artillery fired at the enemy vessels. "An endless fleet lay before our sector," Gockel wrote. "Heavy warships

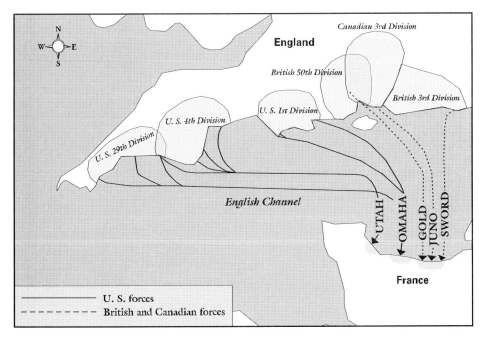

On D-Day, the main American, British, and Canadian army divisions that invaded Normandy stormed across the English Channel from various locations in England.

cruised along as if passing in review. A spectacular but terrifying experience."[7]

The breakfast given to the men of the American 4th Infantry Division was luxurious—steak and eggs, bacon, coffee, and toast. A few men told jokes while they ate. Joking was necessary to cut the tension. At daybreak, the 4th Infantry would hit the beach code-named Utah. No one was certain what kind of defenses awaited them. Some feared they would face a brick wall with a machine gun every twenty yards.

On darkened decks, the soldiers crawled down cargo nets that were draped over the sides of the ships. At the end of the nets they carefully stepped on to Higgins boats, which bobbed furiously in the waves. Then the wait and the terrible seasickness began. Higgins boats are flat-bottomed. The small boats toss in rough water like rubber balls. That wonderful breakfast now burst forth in a mess of undigested eggs and bacon bits. Men packed in the boats had no place to throw up except on each other. Decks became slick with vomit. Many men wept. Some did not care what the Germans had in store for them as long as they could get off the wretched little boats.

The horror of battle exploded before the eyes of the soldiers in the first wave of boats even before they hit the beach. A control ship, the PC 1261, struck a mine and sank in minutes. Crewmen of the PC 1261 swam desperately in the icy waters, pleading to be rescued. Boats could not stop to pick up the swimming men because stopping would make them easy targets

American sailors try to rescue fellow Americans whose landing boats were sunk off the D-Day beaches.

for German guns. Many of the men struggling in the water drowned. A sailor named Sims Gauthier remembered, "Neither I nor anyone that was involved in the actual invasion could stop and pick [the crewmen] up. And this is a sad part to go through, seeing these men screaming, hollering, and asking for help."[8]

Utah Beach was a stretch of yellow sand two hundred to three hundred yards wide and about three miles long. At 6:30 A.M., scores of Higgins boats pushed up to the beach. The ramps dropped, and men of the 4th Infantry Division waded ashore in waist-deep water. Behind the first Higgins boats came waves and waves of others. Thirty thousand men and thirty-five hundred vehicles were slated to land on Utah on the first day.

Once more, a lethal lottery determined the fate of men. Some soldiers encountered terrible German fire on Utah, while others walked in as if they were on a training exercise.

Some soldiers landed under minimum fire or no fire at all. In fact, many climbed up to the beach and saw an elderly American officer—a general—who stood in plain view urging them to move forward. This

SOURCE DOCUMENT

WE WERE LET OFF IN DEEP WATER BEARING HEAVY LOADS OF MORTAR [A MUZZLE-LOADED CANNON] AND MACHINE GUN AMMUNITION WE WERE SUPPOSED TO DEPOSIT ON THE BEACH. WE HAD LIFE PRESERVERS, BUT WHY I DON'T KNOW. IF YOU FELL OVER, THE PRESERVER DIDN'T HELP. THERE WERE MANY BODIES FLOATING BY AND LOTS OF SHOTS BEING FIRED. . . . WHEN I HAD GONE ABOUT A HUNDRED YARDS INLAND, I HEARD CRYING COMING FROM A [SHELL] CRATER. I WENT OVER TO INVESTIGATE AND ONE OF THE MEN FROM MY COMPANY LAY THERE WITH BLOOD SPURTING FROM HIS HIP OR THIGH AREA . . . I CALLED FOR A MEDIC AND WENT LOOKING FOR MY PLATOON. LATER, I FOUND OUT HE HAD DIED AND WAS THE FIRST CASUALTY FROM B COMPANY.[9]

Some soldiers encountered heavy fire at Utah Beach. The Higgins boat carrying Sam Frackman of the 4th Division arrived shortly after the first wave. He describes his experience.

fifty-seven-year-old officer, Theodore Roosevelt, Jr., was the oldest man to land on the invasion beaches at D-Day. When he was a teenager, General Roosevelt had lived in an unusual residence—the White House. He was the eldest son of Theodore Roosevelt, the twenty-sixth president of the United States. The general was also a distant cousin to Franklin Roosevelt, the U.S. president at the time. Now Theodore Roosevelt, Jr., was a respected army officer. He had been with the 4th Division in landing operations in North Africa (1942) and Sicily (1943).

By June 1944, Roosevelt was in poor health with a weak heart and severe arthritis. The general could walk

At Utah Beach, Americans help ashore another group of United States soldiers whose landing craft was sunk. The survivors managed to reach the beach by using a life raft.

only with the aid of a cane. Despite having health problems, Roosevelt insisted on landing with the first wave. In a letter he said his presence was required because, "it will steady the boys to know I am with them."[10] Somehow, he seemed youthful on D-Day morning. With his cane poking in the sand, he trudged up and down the beach, unmindful of the random shellbursts. A sergeant named Harry Brown said he saw Roosevelt, "with a cane in one hand, a map in the other, walking around as if he was looking over some real estate."[11]

Now and then Roosevelt huddled with other officers to study a map. The officers made a troubling discovery. They had landed two thousand yards south of their intended spot. Evidently, the smoke and dust stirred up by naval artillery fire confused the landing craft pilots. What should the 4th Infantry Division do? Should they march laterally along the beach so they could move inland according to plans? Roosevelt dismissed that idea. He said to a colonel, "We're going to start the war from here."[12]

It is now known that the 4th Division's landing at the wrong place was a lucky accident. Had the men approached the shore at their proper landing zone, they would have faced at least two heavy German guns that were dug in on high ground. Roosevelt's decision to march inland from his landing spot saved many lives.

In the opening hours of the invasion, it became evident that not all the enemy troops were the tough and fanatical fighters typical of the German army. In fact, some were not even German. Captain John Ahearn commanded one of the first tanks to land on Utah. Ahearn spotted a German bunker and fired at it. Almost immediately, the defenders came out holding their hands high in the air. Not only were they eager to surrender, they shouted a warning at Ahearn, "*Achtung Meinen!*"[13] (German words for "Watch out for the mines!") The supposed Germans had saved an American tank from being blown up.

Ahearn questioned the men and found that they were from the Soviet Union and they were forced to wear German uniforms. More foreign troops—Poles, Russians, and Lithuanians—were captured on D-Day. The foreigners were prisoners of war who had been captured in previous battles. They were given a choice: Either fight with the German army or die of slow starvation in prisoner-of-war (POW) camps. Of course, the foreigners who chose to fight did not have their hearts in the battle. In one sector, a dozen non-Germans walked toward American lines carrying suitcases they had packed weeks before.

The German high command was forced to use the foreigners because by 1944 their best troops were either dead or wounded or were fighting in the Soviet Union. Moreover, German leaders concluded they did not require first-rate troops to sit behind thick-walled bunkers and fire at an exposed enemy. Even some of the all-German units stationed in Normandy were composed of older men. Those older men had been

SOURCE DOCUMENT

As we pushed inland from Utah I was sent ahead to check the road we were going along . . . after I cleared the corner I suddenly knew someone had their sights on me. I could just feel it. I was about to dive to the ditch when this voice—in the other ditch—said, "Hey soldier, can you give me a light?" A head popped up slightly, and it was grinning. I wasn't sure for a moment whether it was a German playing a trick, but . . . his voice was pure Bronx. He was 101st Airborne, and walked his way towards the beach through the night and morning.[14]

About four hours after the landings, the infantrymen marching inland from Utah Beach began meeting airborne troops who had dropped behind the beaches the night before. Here is an account of PFC P. J. McCall (a soldier in the 4th Infantry Division) meeting an unnamed paratrooper near Utah Beach.

weakened in body and spirit by combat in the Soviet Union. But as the Allies discovered, other sectors of the Normandy front were manned by superb German troops. The quality of German soldiers—like the Atlantic Wall itself—was woefully uneven.

The invasion of Utah Beach suffered what commanders call light casualties. At the end of the day, fewer than two hundred men were killed or wounded and sixty were listed as missing.[15] Most of the missing presumably drowned in waters off the beachhead. As cold as these casualty figures seem, they were indeed "light" compared to other American battles fought that day. Casualty totals were frightening at a tiny peninsula near Utah.

Pointe du Hoc

Jutting out of the Normandy coast was an arrow-shaped point of land called Pointe du Hoc. Allied leaders believed Pointe du Hoc contained at least six large guns hidden in thick concrete emplacements. The 155-millimeter guns propelled a 95-pound shell a distance of twelve miles. They could be pointed at Utah Beach, at Omaha Beach, or at Allied ships. Before the invasion, Pointe du Hoc was pounded by huge bombs. To this day the surface of the small peninsula is scarred by bomb craters that look like circular swimming pools.

At daybreak, some two hundred twenty-five Americans of 2nd Ranger Battalion approached Pointe du Hoc on Higgins boats. Cliffs on Pointe du Hoc rose straight up to the height of a five-story building. There was no approach to this natural fortress other than from the sea. The only way to destroy the German guns was to climb the sheer cliffs. The Ranger attack would be a throwback to medieval times, when invaders had to scale castle walls to reach their enemy inside. Casualties were expected to be heavy.

Firing from the tops of the cliffs, German machine guns and mortars raked the Higgins boats. Many boats were wrecked in the water. Rangers were forced to jump over the sides and swim or wade to the narrow beach that ringed the peninsula. A Ranger named Donald Scribner said:

I remember dropping three different times. Each time I did, machine guns burst in front of my face in the sand. I didn't stop because I knew what was coming; I dropped because I was so tired. I looked back, and saw [my good friend] Walter Geldon lying on the beach with his hand raised up asking for help. Walter never made it. He died on his third wedding anniversary.[16]

Once on the beach, the Rangers hugged the cliffs where they were safe from machine-gun fire but not from the hand grenades and mortar rounds that rained down upon them. Already casualties were high, and the men had yet to climb the forbidding cliffs. Their task seemed impossible. Ten years later, the Ranger

A German bunker at Pointe du Hoc, France, is a tourist attraction today.

commander, Colonel James Rudder, visited Pointe du Hoc with a writer. The colonel said, "Will you tell me how we did this? Anybody would be a fool to try this. It was crazy then, and it's crazy now."[17]

The Rangers were equipped with devices to enable them to scale the cliffsides. Four amphibious trucks (called DUKWs) were fitted with extension ladders borrowed from the London Fire Department. However, one of those DUKWs was sunk by enemy fire. The other three could not get close enough to rest their ladders on the cliffs. The men also had rocket-powered grappling hooks, which trailed climbing ropes. The hooks were designed to catch on objects at the top. But the ropes were heavy from seawater spray. When the hooks were fired, the rocket bases sank into the sand—thereby diminishing their flight.

Disregarding the setbacks, the Rangers continued their attack. A few of the rocket-powered hooks reached the top. Like spiders going up webs, the Rangers began to inch up the cliffs. One Ranger, Sergeant William Stivison, climbed up the fire department ladder and opened up on the Germans with his light machine gun. Sergeant Stivison managed this feat even though the ladder was swaying crazily in the air, unsupported by anything.

Hand by hand, Rangers made their way upward. For many the climb lasted fifteen minutes, but it seemed to take forever. Furious German machine-gun fire greeted the Rangers when they reached the surface of Pointe du Hoc. The men crawled forward and took cover in bomb craters. Once they got their bearings, they looked about to find the gun emplacements they were ordered to destroy. They also made a shocking discovery. The bunkers were empty! Unbeknownst to the Americans, Field Marshal Rommel had ordered the guns to be moved just days earlier. The big guns were replaced by telephone poles, which now stuck out of the concrete bunkers.

At first, the men felt crushed knowing they had bled and died over a string of empty bunkers. Yet their mission proved vital to Allied success at D-Day. When machine-gun fire subsided, two Rangers, Leonard Lomell and Jack Kuhn, followed a path. The path appeared to have been used recently to drag heavy equipment. In a remarkable fortune of war, they discovered the guns dug-in and well-camouflaged on a farmer's field. Amazingly, German crews were far to the side eating breakfast. They had left the guns unguarded. Lomell and Kuhn stole up to the guns and destroyed them by placing thermite grenades into their breech mechanisms. Thermite grenades burn white hot and fuse metal parts together. In this manner, the massive artillery pieces, which were pointed toward Utah Beach, were rendered useless.

The destruction of the guns did not end the battle of Pointe du Hoc. The peninsula lay only three miles west of Omaha Beach. German forces launched brutal counterattacks in an effort to drive the men off their newly won ground. The Ranger casualty rate was one of the highest of any units on D-Day. At the end of the day, only about ninety of the two hundred twenty-five men who began the operation were still capable of fighting.[18]

The British and Canadian Beaches

Taken together Sword, Juno, and Gold Beaches were about twenty miles long. The three beaches were assigned to the British, the Canadians, and other forces fighting for the United Kingdom. As was true with the Americans on Utah, the United Kingdom soldiers met deadly resistance in some sections and had relatively easy going in others.

Bill Bidmead of the British Commandos rode on a landing craft, which struck a mine just yards from his beach. The blast caused the front end of the landing craft to jut high in the air. "We were practically vertical," Bidmead remembered. "I found myself under a pile of chaps [men] and also held down by my ninety-pound [field pack]. As we crashed down, the ramp was kicked open. The first chap out was practically ripped in half by bursts of machine gun fire."[19] In sharp contrast to Bidmead's ordeal was the experience of British commando Arnold Wheeldon, who came in nearby. "We got off in water up to our chests. . . . What surprised me was the lack of any carnage on our beach. In our particular sector, there was not a lot of ground shelling from gun emplacements."[20]

The United Kingdom troops benefited by having tanks land almost alongside the infantry. Special swimming tanks called DDs (Direct Drive tanks) were made for this invasion. The DDs were basically American-made Sherman tanks that were fitted with an inner-tubelike flotation device and provided with two propellers. A direct drive shaft from the motor gave the propellers power. Even under ideal conditions, the DDs sank easily and were difficult to steer through waves. British naval leaders determined that the waters were far too choppy for long-distance DD operations, so they brought the amphibious tanks as close to the beaches as their landing craft could manage. This proved to be a fortunate move.

The British had a score to settle. Early in the war, their people suffered devastating bombing raids and lived in fear of a German invasion. The British would never forget the sting of defeat when their armies were driven off the continent at Dunkirk in 1941. The Canadians wished to avenge their failed 1942 raid at the French port city of Dieppe. The men coming in at the United Kingdom beaches were well trained, well equipped, and eager to pay back the Germans for the miseries they caused.

The deadliest fighting took place on Juno Beach, the middle of the three United Kingdom beaches. The first obstacle faced by the men of the 3rd Canadian Division was the hundreds of mines cleverly laid by Rommel's engineers. Scores of landing craft were wrecked in the water either by mines or shellfire. The sea was strewn with men swimming desperately, weighted down by their heavy packs. Many Canadian soldiers drowned before reaching the beach.

On shore, a murderous crossfire cut down the attacking Canadians. Initial fighting on Juno Beach was as lethal as anywhere else on D-Day. Machine-gun bullets poured out of well-concealed bunkers. Barbed wire, mines, and beach obstacles barred the Canadian advance. But unlike nearby Omaha, Juno Beach was relatively flat. There were no high bluffs on which the Germans could hide and fire down at the attackers. Canadian soldiers from the first few waves of boats pushed forward and drove the Germans off the beach. Subsequent waves landed suffering little enemy fire.

By the end of the day on June 6, the Canadians at Juno had joined the British on Gold Beach to their right. Only a narrow strip of land now separated them from Sword Beach. Casualties at Juno Beach were grave: twelve hundred men—one out of every eighteen who landed at Juno—was either killed or wounded.[21]

A landing boat unloads its troops on the coast of France on June 6, 1944.

BLOODY OMAHA

Within ten minutes of the [Higgins boat] ramps being lowered, A Company had become inert, leaderless, and almost incapable of action. Every officer and sergeant had been killed or wounded. . . . The men in the water pushed wounded men ashore, and those who had reached the sands crawled back into the water pulling others to land to save them from drowning. . . . Within twenty minutes of striking the beach A Company had ceased to be an assault company and had become a forlorn little rescue party bent upon survival and saving lives.[1]

—Official report of A Company,
116th Infantry Regiment.

Today, Omaha Beach is a pleasant spot to stroll or to swim in the Channel waters. However, everyone taking a holiday here is mindful of its terrible history. Three pyramid-shaped beach obstacles, now moved to one side, attract the attention of tourists. A German bunker with concrete walls more than two feet thick remains as a token of this spot's bloody past.

At low tide, Omaha is about three hundred yards wide. Above the beach are bluffs—almost sheer

A tour guide stands alongside a pyramid-shaped beach obstacle on Omaha Beach today.

cliffs—which rise some one hundred feet. This type of terrain is a paradise for a defender and a hell for an attacker. Defenders holding high ground enjoy a commanding view over any soldiers coming in from the sea. In 1944, the bluffs above Omaha were lined with well-camouflaged machine-gun nests. From these emplacements, German gunners fired downward with deadly precision on troops at the waterline. Men hitting the beach were virtually defenseless against enemy bullets and artillery.

Omaha Beach is six miles long with towering cliffs on both ends. It was obvious to the Germans that if the Allies were to attack in the Normandy area, Omaha

Beach would be a prime landing spot. The job to take Omaha was given to the American 1st and 29th Infantry divisions supported by several Ranger companies. Some forty thousand men and thirty-five hundred vehicles were scheduled to land on Omaha at D-Day. In 1944, Omaha was the site of one of the most horrible battles in the history of the U.S. Army.

H-Hour

The men waiting to land gazed at Omaha Beach, awed by the furious barrage. First, low-flying bombers pounded the shore. Then, the big guns from dozens of warships poured in shell after shell. All of Omaha Beach seemed to be in flames. Some of the troops believed this landing would be a walk-in. Nothing could possibly live through a bombardment such as this. But, as students of this battle would later note, the bombers hit too far inland to effectively destroy German gunners near the beach. The naval barrage, though ferocious, was too brief. Also, the Germans were superbly dug-in. Despite the breathtaking power of the Allied shore bombardment, hundreds of enemy guns remained manned and ready.

Just after 6 A.M., the two hundred boats making up the first wave bored in: eight hundred yards, seven hundred yards, six hundred yards. No German fire. Then, when the lead boats were about four hundred yards from land, the beach earned its nickname: Bloody Omaha. Mortars, artillery, and machine-gun fire rained down on the landing craft. The slow-moving boats made perfect targets for German gunners. One German machine gunner, interviewed twenty years after the battle, said in broken English, "It was the first time I shoot at living men. I don't remember exactly how it was; the only thing I know is that I went to my machine gun and I shoot, I shoot, I shoot."[2]

Landing craft rammed into beach obstacles and sandbars, forcing the men to climb over the sides and swim for shore. Many landing boats struck underwater mines and blew up. Waters on the shoreline turned pink with blood. Sergeant Barton A. Davis, who had made it to the beach, looked back to see a landing craft filled with troops explode: "I saw black dots of men trying to swim through the gasoline that had spread on the water and as we wondered what to do a headless torso flew a good fifty feet through the air and landed with a sickening thud near us."[3]

Boats hitting the beach were raked with machine-gun fire as soon as their ramps dropped. In some cases, all the men aboard the Higgins boat were killed or wounded before they even stepped on enemy shore. Sergeant Harry Bare led his men off a boat into this hellish crossfire: "We waded to the sand and threw ourselves down and the men were frozen, unable to move. My radioman had his head blown off three yards from me. The beach was covered with bodies, men with no legs, no arms—God it was awful."[4]

There was no cover—nowhere to hide from the murderous fire. DD tanks, which were supposed to land with the infantry, were nowhere to be found. In a costly decision, navy commanders sent the DDs into the waters more than a mile away from the beach. This distance was too far for the clumsy DDs to navigate in choppy seas. Many of the tanks sank like rocks, carrying their crews with them to the bottom. Of the twenty-nine DD tanks assigned to Omaha, only two made it to the beach.

The horror of this battle—the exploding shells, the screams of the wounded, the whine of bullets—was a whirlpool engulfing all the attackers. Behind the men was the sea, already crowded with drowned or drowning soldiers. Ahead were a few hundred yards of sand, strewn with obstacles and barbed wire. Unseen land mines were buried everywhere. "Boys were turned into men," said infantryman Bob Slaughter. "Some would be very brave men; others would soon be dead men, but any who survived would be frightened men. Some wet their pants, others cried unashamedly."[5] A PFC from the 1st Infantry Division remembered, "There were men crying with fear, men defecating themselves. I lay there with some others, too petrified to move. . . . It was like a mass paralysis."[6]

Soldiering On

Somehow—with almost inhuman courage—small groups of soldiers pushed away from the waterline and toward enemy positions on the bluffs. Officers and sergeants led the way. Colonel George Taylor found bunches of men huddling together, motionless with fear. Taylor shouted to them, "There are only two

Wounded American soldiers of the 16th Infantry Regiment wait to be evacuated from Omaha Beach.

kinds of people on this beach: the dead and those about to die. So let's get the hell out of here."[7] Most often, it was the platoon leaders and company commanders who organized the soldiers and moved them forward. Sergeant John Ellery said, "I didn't see any generals in my area of the beach, but I did see a captain and two lieutenants who demonstrated courage beyond belief as they struggled to bring order to the chaos around them."[8]

To clear paths in barbed wire, the Americans used Bangalore torpedoes. Bangalores, nicknamed "stovepipes," were tubular explosive charges made in sections three feet long. Men crawled to the barbed wire, screwed the sections together, and slid the devices under the wire entanglement. The Bangalores blew up the wire and detonated any land mines buried under the sand.

The naval gunfire aided infantrymen struggling on the beach. Commanding the ships off Omaha was Rear Admiral C. F. Bryant, who served aboard the battleship *Texas*. Bryant got on his radio and shouted to the ships under his command, "Get on them, men! Get on them! They're raising hell with the men on the beach, and we can't have any more of that! We must stop it!"[9]

Big-gunned vessels such as the *Texas* were too far offshore to see German gun positions through the smoke of battle. The huge ships lay so low in the water they could not sail closer to the shore, or they would run aground and become stationary targets for German artillery. This situation left fire support up to the destroyers, the smallest warships in the U.S. fleet. As the battle raged, the "tin cans," as the destroyers were called, sailed so close to shore their keels [ship bottoms] rubbed the seafloor.

With most of their radios lost, the infantry found novel means to communicate with the destroyers and direct their fire. A lone tank on Omaha fired at a German-held cliffside. Then a head popped up out of the tank and a crewman waved to the destroyer *Carmick*, which lay some five hundred yards offshore. Clearly, the tank crewman wanted the *Carmick* to fire where he had just fired. The *Carmick* complied. The tank then shifted its revolving turret and fired again. Once more, the *Carmick* repeated its action. This wordless communication between tank and ship continued and destroyed many German gun positions.[10]

In the opening hours of battle, the tin-can destroyers provided the infantry's only artillery support. Even though German guns fired at the small ships, they sailed dangerously close to the beach, seeking out gun emplacements (called pillboxes). A sailor named O'Neill remembered:

> The destroyers were firing their 5-inch shells pointblank at the pillboxes; you could see the shells as they went screaming overhead and smacked against the concrete walls. They bounced skyward off the sloping sides of those pillboxes, but they managed to get a few of them into the gun ports. The enemy fire soon stopped.[11]

Army and navy medics who tended to the wounded became saints in the eyes of the infantry. On the exposed beach, the medics gave first aid to terribly wounded men even as bullets slammed at them. Stretcher-bearers wove through machine-gun fire to bring badly wounded men to the shore, where Higgins boats evacuated them to hospital ships. A sailor named Ferris Burke, who served on a hospital ship, said:

> The doctors were outstanding. Just unbelievable. They worked for hours, amputating arms and legs, removing shrapnel [fragments from exploding shells], patching bullet wounds, and trying to calm down some men who were completely out of their minds.[12]

Waves and waves of landing craft continued to bring fresh troops and supplies to Omaha Beach. One of the men present was Hollywood movie director John Ford, who was there to preserve this historic battle on film. Ford noticed an African-American soldier unloading a landing craft despite shells bursting around him. The services were segregated in those days, with blacks and whites assigned to separate units. African-American soldiers were often only assigned supply duties. Ford said:

Fellow soldiers placed crossed rifles on the beach as a sign of respect for this dead American.

> I remember watching one colored man in an [amphibious truck] loaded with supplies. He dropped them on the beach, unloaded, went back for more. . . . Shells landed around him. The Germans were really after him. He avoided every obstacle and just kept going back and forth, back and forth. I thought, By God, if anybody deserves a medal that man does.[13]

Land mines are one of the greatest nightmares any infantryman can face. Knowing one's next step may be one's last step will cower even the bravest soldier. Buried in the sands of Omaha were wooden mines, which escaped the scrutiny of magnetic mine detectors. A particularly cruel mine, nicknamed the Bouncing Betty, had two charges. The first charge blew a bomb in the air about waist high. The second charge exploded the bomb, sending deadly shrapnel into anyone nearby.

General Rommel was keenly aware of the terror generated by land mines. He insisted that mines be planted liberally throughout the beach area. The Americans at Omaha had no choice but to overcome their dread and clear lanes in the minefields. With many of their mine detectors lost at landing, this had to be done the slow and painful way. Troops on their bellies, moving like snakes, probed the sands ahead of them with their bayonets. The men clearing lanes through the minefields trailed bands of special white tape behind them. The tape told soldiers in the rear they would be safe to walk through here as long as they stepped on the tape. Scores of mine-clearers paid with their lives. Captain Joseph Dawson wrote, "[My company] proceeded off of a beach through a minefield which had been identified by some of the soldiers who had landed earlier. We knew this because two of them were lying there in the path I selected. Both men had been destroyed by the mines."[14]

Slowly, the invaders closed to the bluffs that rose above the sands of Omaha. The fight for Omaha Beach was one of the few battles where men sought safety by going forward instead of to the rear. The bluffs ahead presented difficult angles for German gunners, whereas a soldier on the exposed beach was an easy target. In its later stages, the battle focused on the gaps of these bluffs.

Infantrymen near the bluffs caught their first sight of the enemy. Private H. W. Shroeder saw a line of German prisoners being led down the bluff and noted, "[They] were really roughed up. Their hair was full of cement, dirt, everything. They didn't look so tough. So we started up the bluff carrying our stuff, and others started following us."[15]

The men at Omaha also encountered non-German soldiers. At one point, Major William Washington saw two American privates leading fifty captured troops down the bluffs. Washington asked the obvious question: How did two men capture fifty? The two explained that they were both of Polish heritage, and they were captured early in the battle. They soon discovered that their captors were Polish prisoners of war who were forced to fight for the Germans. Speaking to their captors in Polish, the two infantrymen persuaded the enemy soldiers to surrender to the Americans.[16]

After six hours of terrible combat, the American infantry at Omaha held a beachhead about six miles long and two miles deep at its broadest point. Artillery and mortar fire still harassed the American forces. The Omaha invaders had suffered three thousand killed, wounded, and missing. Everyone feared a counterattack by German tanks. In their weakened condition, the men would have been unable to resist any kind of strong German offensive. One American remembered, "They could have swept us off with a broom."[17] But the enemy counterattack never came. Instead, supplies and reinforcements flowed onto the beach.

More hospital work— lots of blood. I am sorry for the men, all shot away and encased with plaster [yet they are] so willing to tease and laugh at [a nurse] who is trying to help. . . .[1]

—Miss C.S.M. Petrie, a British army nurse who tended to the wounded in the days after D-Day.

THE BATTLE OF NORMANDY

All was quiet the morning of June 6 at Adolf Hitler's mountain retreat in the German region of Bavaria. Hitler's military advisor, General Alfred Jodl, had received telephone reports telling of an Allied invasion at Normandy. His boss had taken a sleeping pill and was sound asleep. Hitler customarily slept until noon every day. If Jodl woke the German chief early, the man would fly into a rage. Everyone who worked at headquarters dreaded Hitler's all-too-frequent temper tantrums. So, Jodl decided to let his commander sleep. News of the invasion would have to wait.

The German Reaction

At ten in the morning, the phone rang at the home of Field Marshal Erwin Rommel. He was visiting his wife in the German town of Ulm. It was Frau Rommel's

After the beaches are secure, thousands of Allied troops land at Normandy.

fiftieth birthday, and the field marshal had presented her with a pair of red shoes he had bought at an expensive Paris shop. Two days earlier, Rommel had determined that he could afford to take a quick vacation because of the stormy weather over the English Channel. The Allies, he believed, would never invade in such turbulence. When told that large-scale landings had taken place in Normandy, he hung up the phone and said, "How stupid of me. How stupid of me."[2] Frau Rommel later recalled, "The call changed him . . . there was a terrible tension."[3]

The only German commander in France was Gerd von Rundstedt, the sixty-nine-year-old field marshal. Upon hearing the news, Rundstedt ordered two German armored divisions to head for Normandy. The two divisions included more than three hundred tanks and thousands of soldiers. However, the armored divisions never moved because they were not Rundstedt's to command. Hitler insisted that the decision to move tanks anywhere on the coast of France belong only to him. And on D-Day, Adolf Hitler was asleep.

The Germans made no massive counterattack against the D-Day invaders. Confusion at the top between Hitler, Von Rundstedt, and Rommel was the

SOURCE DOCUMENT

I WOULD SAY WE WERE READY TO MARCH AT 2 A.M. AT THE LATEST. . . . THE ENGINES OF THE TANKS WERE RUNNING, BUT WE DIDN'T RECEIVE ANY MARCHING ORDERS. WE THOUGHT, "IF WE HAVE TO MARCH, LET'S GO NOW WHILE IT'S DARK AND THE ENEMY PLANES CAN'T SEE US." WE WAITED FOR ORDERS AND WE WAITED. JUST STOOD THERE, INACTIVE BY OUR TANKS. WE COULDN'T UNDERSTAND WHY WE WEREN'T GETTING ANY ORDERS AT ALL.[4]

Men of the German 21st Panzer (tank) Division were poised and ready to move to Normandy when they first heard of the airborne assaults. An assault by this panzer division could have done grave damage to allied paratroopers and to men on the beaches. A German tank crewman named Werner Kortenhaus wondered why his unit was not told to attack.

major reason for the inaction. The French Resistance, a brave band of civilians, also worked through the night sabotaging railroad tracks and cutting telephone lines. The French men and women who fought their German occupiers were loosely directed by Allied leaders in London. If captured, Resistance members faced torture and execution at the hands of the Germans. Yet on D-Day night, men and women of the Resistance boldly disrupted lines of communication between German troops on the coast and their headquarters units farther inland.

Hitler finally rose from bed at noon, as usual. He was told about the attack at Normandy. Immediately he thought the Normandy invasion was a feint designed to make the Germans shift their armored divisions to the south. The German leader predicted the real invasion would come at the Pas-de-Calais. There, the Allies would encounter the strongest fortifications in the Atlantic Wall. Most important, German tanks must remain near the Pas-de-Calais region. There would be no counterattack with tanks at Normandy. The German chief seemed delighted at the prospects of an overwhelming victory. "The news couldn't be better," Hitler said.[5]

Celebration

At 9:30 A.M., British time, General Eisenhower's press aide made a brief announcement: "Under the command of General Eisenhower, Allied naval forces, supported by strong air forces, began landing Allied armies this morning on the northern coast of France."[6] The news was electric. Men and women walking the London streets cheered as if at a football game. Londoners stopped American servicepeople, shook their hands, and hugged them. In factories throughout Great Britain, workers stood and sang their national anthem, "God Save the King." The second front was finally established. A war-weary British public now believed this terrible conflict would soon be over.

In the United States, the announcement was first heard on the East Coast at 3:30 A.M. and at 12:39 A.M. on the West Coast. In wartime America, millions toiled on factory night shifts assembling ships and planes. Word of the invasion was announced on factory loudspeakers. Night-shift workers applauded. Freight trains blew their whistles and motorists pressed car horns. In Norfolk, Virginia, a baby girl, born early on June 6, was given the first name Dee Day by her mother.

There was no home television in those days, but in the morning bold newspaper headlines told of the invasion. "ALLIED ARMIES LAND IN FRANCE. . . . GREAT INVASION IS UNDER WAY,"[7] said a *New York Times* extra edition, which hit the streets at 6:00 A.M.

The American Home Front

Wartime Americans identified themselves as soldiers who served on what was called the home front. The solemn duty of Americans at home was to produce the war goods needed on the fighting fronts. Home-front America was a blend of patriotism, frenzied work, and war nerves. Just about everyone had a relative or friend serving in the armed forces. People followed shifting battle lines on maps as closely as they watched baseball scores. Now, they looked upon D-Day as the war-winning effort that would bring victory at last. Radio announcers talked about little else save the strike on French soil. Baseball games were cancelled on June 6. Theaters on New York's Broadway closed their doors for one day. Church bells tolled throughout the land. Even America's most treasured bell—the Liberty Bell in Philadelphia—was given a gentle tap.

Women did much of the dirty and the monotonous work in home-front factories. The symbol of American industrial strength was "Rosie the Riveter." Rosie was pictured on wartime posters as a muscular yet attractive lady who was ready to do her part in winning the war. She represented the 18 million U.S. women who took industrial jobs during the war years. The armed forces were rigidly separated at the time. Women served in all-women units, which were usually kept far from the front lines. But if American women could not participate in battle, they were eager to serve in the factories. The Higgins Company, which produced the vital Higgins boats, employed thousands of women workers. Without the aid of home-front women, the D-Day invasion could not have been launched.

D-Day was the nation's greatest gamble so far in the war. Casualties were likely to be staggering. Thus,

June 6 was a day of prayer on the home front. In a busy Brooklyn shipyard, workers dropped to their knees and together said the Lord's Prayer. In small towns, the lights of churches were the first lights to go on that morning. In Coffeyville, Kansas, families still in their pajamas knelt on their front porches. Most Americans read the D-Day prayer offered by President Franklin Roosevelt:

> Almighty God: Our sons, pride of our nation, this day have set upon a mighty endeavor, a struggle to preserve our Republic, our religion, and our civilization, and to set free a suffering humanity. Lead them straight and true; give strength to their arms, stoutness to their hearts, steadfastness in their faith. . . .[8]

After sunset on June 6, New York City residents looked to their waterfront to see the lights on the Statue of Liberty shining brightly. This was an astonishing sight. Since the start of the war, the floodlights that normally bathe the statue at night had been turned off to conform to the city's blackout codes. Lurking German submarines could see ships against the background of street lights, so all East Coast cities dimmed their lights to deny submarines their prey. Now the Statue of Liberty's lights not only burned, they also blinked out a message: dot, dot, dot, dash. Most home front Americans knew this was Morse Code for the letter V—V for Victory.

Beyond the Beaches

Before darkness fell on June 6, some one hundred seventy-five thousand paratroopers and amphibious soldiers were in Normandy. Overall, the United States casualties on D-Day totaled 3,393 killed and 3,210 wounded. No one knows the number of German casualties on D-Day, but estimates range between four thousand and nine thousand. By the end of June, Field Marshal Rommel claimed he had lost some two hundred fifty thousand men.

Tons of military equipment and vehicles are unloaded on the Normandy beaches in preparation for the push through France to Germany.

Allied beaches on June 7 looked as if they were locked in big-city traffic jams. Trucks, tanks, and heavy guns rolled off landing ships and headed inland. For every five men put ashore on D-Day, one combat vehicle was also delivered to the beaches. All along the front, dozens of linkups had been made between ground forces and paratroopers. The important Normandy town of Bayeux was taken by British ground troops on the evening of June 7. German prisoners were being rounded up by the hundreds.

The beachheads were far from secure the day after D-Day. Artillery and sniper fire hampered crews unloading boats. Minefields still had to be cleared. An

---

SOURCE DOCUMENT

AFTER THE OMAHA BEACH MASSACRE, I VOWED NEVER TO TAKE A GERMAN PRISONER. [THEN I FOUND A WOUNDED GERMAN SOLDIER.] MY FIRST REACTION WAS TO PUT HIM OUT OF HIS MISERY. I BELIEVE HE SENSED WHAT I WAS THINKING. HE SAID, TEARFULLY, "*BITTE* [PLEASE]." HE WAS AN IMPRESSIVE LOOKING SOLDIER AND I JUST COULDN'T DO IT. AS I DEPARTED, HE SMILED WEAKLY, AND SAID IN GUTTURAL ENGLISH, "DANKE VERY MUCH, MAY GOTT BLESS YOU. GUT LUCK." THAT CHANGED MY MIND. I STILL HATED THE GERMAN SOLDIER, BUT I COULDN'T KILL ONE AT CLOSE RANGE IF HIS HANDS WERE OVER HIS HEAD.[9]

In the heat of battle, hatred sometimes rules a soldier's mind, prompting him to commit atrocities such as killing prisoners. But humanity can also emerge, as this report by Bob Slaughter of the American 29th Infantry Division points out.

enemy-held gap separated Omaha from Utah Beach. It was not until June 12, six days after the invasion, that all five Allied beaches were joined. The merger meant Allied forces now owned more than fifty miles of uninterrupted Normandy coastline. By July 2, about 2 million troops and two hundred fifty thousand vehicles had landed in France. The second front was well established.

Soldiers and sailors waged a war of supply. The average infantry divisions of fifteen thousand men required five hundred tons of supplies a day to keep it in operation. Five infantry divisions came ashore in the first week. Bringing supplies from England to Normandy presented a stupendous challenge to Allied engineers. The English Channel is plagued with treacherous currents and high waves. Cargo ships must nestle in inlets or ports to find the calm waters needed for unloading. However, the Normandy shores had no natural ports to serve large-scale cargo operations. So, the Allies brought their ports with them with two remarkable devices called Mulberry harbors.

The Mulberries were gigantic breakwaters, or barriers that protect a shore from waves. They were made in England and floated in sections across the channel. More than one million tons of concrete and steel went into the two structures. Each artificial pier was larger in surface area than New York City's Central Park. Some twenty thousand British workers toiled in the utmost secrecy to create the Mulberries. Once in place on the Normandy shores, they served brilliantly. Ships tied alongside a Mulberry and off-loaded vehicles, ammunition, food, medical supplies, and other war goods. At their peak, each Mulberry handled twenty-five hundred vehicles a day.

Nature, not the Germans, dealt a blow to the Allied war of supply. On June 19, the worst storm in forty years struck the English Channel. For three days, gale-force winds and savage waves lashed the Normandy coast. More Allied ships were damaged and sunk during this storm than were lost to German artillery fire on D-Day. Worst of all, the storm wrecked one of the Mulberry harbors beyond repair. The loss of the breakwater meant that Allied ships would have to bring their supplies directly onto the Normandy beaches as they did at D-Day.

Battle of the Hedgerows

Spreading out from the invasion beaches, the Allies battled stubborn German soldiers in the hedgerow country. For centuries, Normandy farmers had marked their fields by building dirt and stone fences. The fences, known as hedgerows, stood three to five feet high and were about four feet thick. The hedgerows created a vast checkerboard—a maze of walls—on the Normandy landscape. Hedgerows made Normandy an ideal spot for defensive warfare.

German troops placed machine guns and antitank guns behind the hedgerows. The thick earthen barriers absorbed Allied fire and protected the defenders. Allied infantrymen assaulted the hedgerows and took

In Normandy, a rifle and a helmet mark a temporary grave for an American killed on D-Day.

terrible casualties in the process. Even when the Germans retreated, they merely pulled back to the next hedgerow. The Allies were forced to fight bloody battles hedgerow to hedgerow and field to field.

Roads in Normandy consisted of narrow lanes lined by hedgerows. Tanks had to advance in single file rather than in large flanking formations. This made the tanks easy marks for German antitank guns. In Normandy, the Allies also encountered the dreaded German machine known as the Tiger tank. The Tiger was twice the weight of the American-built Sherman tank and it had a more powerful gun. The only way

American tank crews could defeat a Tiger was to attack in packs and try to hit the enemy machine at its side or rear. In the hedgerow country, such movement was often impossible. The out-classed Shermans suffered severe losses.

Capturing the city of Caen was a key to breaking out of the Normandy front. Caen lay eight miles inland from the British beaches. Allied plans called for occupying Caen no later than June 7. However, British General Montgomery was slow to advance on Caen, thereby allowing the Germans to reinforce their garrison in the city. Montgomery's failure to take Caen infuriated American leaders and further disturbed Allied harmony. Once more Dwight Eisenhower—always the diplomat—had to soothe ruffled feelings between American and British leaders.

German defenders in Caen held the city for six weeks. The beautiful city, which was called the "city of a thousand steeples" for its many ornate churches, was flattened by bombs and shells. During the siege, thousands of men, women, and children were killed. All Normandy civilians suffered in the battle for the province, but nowhere was the destruction and the loss of life greater than at Caen.

Hedgerow by hedgerow, the Allies began to win the Battle of Normandy. American ingenuity played a part in the struggle. A sergeant named Culin came up with the simple way to penetrate hedgerows. Culin cut sections of steel into sturdy blades. He welded the sections to the front ends of American tanks. This allowed the tanks to cut through a hedgerow rather than climbing over it and exposing their thin-skinned bottom to enemy fire. Ironically, the steel used to make the cutting blades was salvaged from obstacles the Germans placed on the beaches in an attempt to stop American landings. Dwight Eisenhower claimed Sergeant Culin's device "gave a tremendous boost to morale throughout the Army."[10]

The Battle of Normandy ended on July 25 when the Allies crushed German resistance and began to race across France. In the breakout, sixty thousand German troops were captured or killed. Also in June 1944, the Soviet Union began a powerful offensive. Soviet troops closed in on Germany from the east. Germany was now in the dreaded position of fighting a war on two fronts—and losing on both of them.

*N*one of my comrades who had survived the [D-Day] invasion continued to believe in victory.[1]

—Private Franz Gockel, a German infantryman.

THE AFTERMATH

On June 17, 1944, Adolf Hitler met with Field Marshals Von Rundstedt and Rommel, his two commanders on the western front. The meeting took place inside a bunker in the suburbs of Paris, France. Another man present, General Hans Speidel, said, "He [Hitler] looked pale and sleepless, playing nervously with his glasses and an array of colored pencils which he held between his fingers."[2]

D-Day and German Defeat

Hitler urged his generals to fight the enemy with greater vigor because his new super weapons would soon change the course of the war. Indeed, the first German V-1 rocket-powered missiles hit England on June 13, and the even larger V-2 rocket was almost ready for use. These V, or "vengeance," weapons were capable of hitting targets more than one hundred miles away. But the V-1 and V-2 rockets were terror weapons designed to throw civilians into a state of panic. The

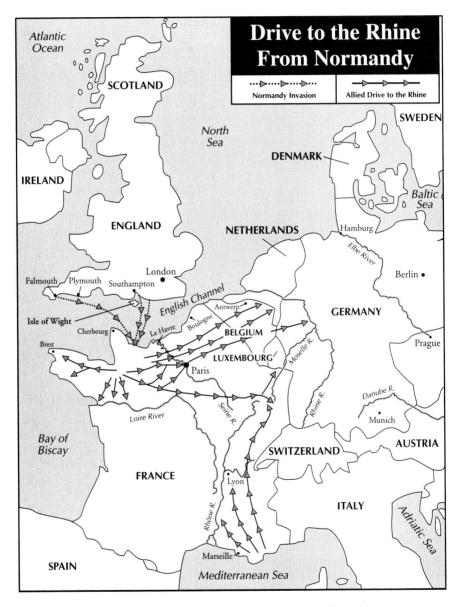

Drive to the Rhine From Normandy

···▷····▷····▷···	→→→
Normandy Invasion	Allied Drive to the Rhine

Atlantic Ocean

SCOTLAND

SWEDEN

North Sea

DENMARK

Baltic Sea

IRELAND

ENGLAND

NETHERLANDS

Hamburg

Elbe River

Berlin •

London

Falmouth   Plymouth   Southampton

English Channel

Antwerp

GERMANY

Prague

Isle of Wight

Cherbourg

Le Havre   Boulogne

BELGIUM

Brest

LUXEMBOURG

Moselle R.

Paris

Loire River

Seine R.

Rhine R.

Danube R.

Munich

Bay of Biscay

SWITZERLAND

AUSTRIA

FRANCE

Lyon

ITALY

Adriatic Sea

Rhône R.

Marseille

SPAIN

Mediterranean Sea

After the D-Day invasion, Allied troops worked to liberate France and then pushed to the Rhine River in Germany. They were now poised to drive toward Berlin.

flying bombs lacked the accuracy to be effective against military targets.

Von Rundstedt and Rommel listened to Hitler with growing impatience. Rommel, who had just arrived from the front and had not slept the night before, became testy. "[T]he struggle was hopeless," said Rommel, "against the [Allied] superiority in the air, at sea, and on the land."[3] Then Rommel suggested the unthinkable—end the war, ask the Allies for peace. Hitler refused even to discuss surrender. He blamed his generals for defeats on the fighting fronts.

The meeting broke up with everyone harboring bitter feelings. Rommel did win a promise for Hitler to visit the troops on the Normandy front lines. Field

American soldiers hold a captured German flag in the town of Chambois, France, in August 1944.

Marshal Rommel believed such a visit from the German supreme commander would boost the men's spirits. Then, hours before Hitler was scheduled to go to the front, a V-1 rocket that was aimed at England made an errant U-turn and exploded dangerously close to Hitler's bunker. A shaken Hitler abruptly cancelled his trip to the front. He took an express train back to Germany and never again stepped on French soil.

Two months after his meeting with Hitler, Field Marshal Erwin Rommel was dead. Rommel thought Hitler was a madman. He hoped getting rid of Hitler would end the war and save German lives. He was implicated in a July 1944 attempt to assassinate Hitler. Rommel was given his choice to commit suicide by drinking poison or face a trial that could embarrass and injure his family. He chose suicide. Hitler escaped assassination and the war continued. On April 30, 1945, Adolf Hitler committed suicide in his Berlin bunker. A week later, Germany surrendered to the Allies.

Germany's defeat was made inevitable by D-Day and the establishment of a second front in Western Europe. Most Germans knew their country could not fight a war on two fronts and hope to win. Hitler held out until the last moment because he wanted to save his own neck. He was well aware the victorious Allies would demand his execution for war crimes. His war crimes included the execution of prisoners and the systematic slaughter of Europe's Jews. (This slaughter of the Jews was later called the Holocaust.) The continuance

Americans of the 4th Infantry Division view the Eiffel Tower after the Allies liberated Paris in late August 1944.

of the war was costly for Hitler's enemies. From D-Day until Germany surrendered eleven months later, many bloody battles were fought and many thousands of Allied soldiers lost their lives in Europe.

Reflections on D-Day

Above Omaha Beach today spreads the American Normandy Cemetery. Here, on the bluff where the

In London, British civilians and American soldiers celebrate Germany's surrender in May 1945.

Germans once had trenches and gun emplacements, are graves of more than nine thousand American soldiers. One of the graves holds General Theodore Roosevelt, Jr., who led the invasion of Utah Beach and died of a heart attack two weeks later. Roosevelt was awarded the Congressional Medal of Honor for his courage and leadership on D-Day.

Walking amid the nine thousand crosses and Stars of David at the American Normandy Cemetery is a solemn and a moving experience. Many of the

Americans resting here were killed in battle within a month of the June 6, 1944, invasion. The gravemarkers do not give birthdates, but a casual visitor will notice that about half the graves are those of privates and PFCs. The average private or PFC was nineteen years old.

D-Day was a victory for the forces of freedom in 1944. But in war, triumph is always married to tragedy. At the American Normandy Cemetery lies the true and painful aftermath of D-Day and World War II. So many young men—barely out of high school—died

The American Normandy Cemetery as it looks today. The cemetery was built on the bluffs overlooking Omaha Beach and holds more than nine thousand graves.

an ocean away from their homes. So many families mourned back in the United States.

Still, D-Day—June 6, 1944—will always be remembered as one of the single most important days in the twentieth century. It was a day of victory for the forces of freedom. Twenty years after the invasion, Dwight Eisenhower visited the D-Day sites. Before the war, Eisenhower had been an army colonel who was ready to quietly retire after thirty years of service. He was virtually unknown to the American public. At war's end, Eisenhower was one of the country's greatest heroes. He became so popular the American people elected him president in 1952 and again in 1956.

When he toured Normandy in 1964, Eisenhower stood on Omaha Beach and told TV reporter Walter Cronkite, "[I]t's a wonderful thing to remember what those fellows twenty years ago were fighting for. . . . Not to conquer any territory, not for any ambitions of our own, but to make sure that Hitler could not destroy freedom in the world."[4]

★ TIMELINE ★

1918—World War I ends; Germany is the major defeated power.

1919—The World War I peace treaty, called the Treaty of Versailles, is signed; The treaty reduces Germany's size by one-eighth and abolishes its army and navy.

1933—Adolf Hitler comes to power in Germany; He vows to defy the Treaty of Versailles and begins to build up the German military.

1939—*September 1*: German troops invade Poland, thereby starting World War II.
September 3: Britain and France, allies of Poland, declare war on Germany.
September 27: The city of Warsaw, capital of Poland, surrenders to the Germans.

1940—*April 9*: Germany invades Denmark and Norway.
May 10: Germany attacks Belgium, Luxembourg, and The Netherlands.
May 29: British and French troops are trapped at the port city of Dunkirk; Some 336,000 troops are eventually rescued.
June 22: France surrenders to Germany.
September 7: London suffers heavy damage from bombs as the air war called the Battle of Britain begins.

1941—*June 22*: Germany invades the Soviet Union.
December 7: Japan attacks the American naval base at Pearl Harbor, Hawaii.

December 8: The United States declares war on Japan.

December 11: Germany declares war on the United States.

1942—*November 7–8*: U. S. forces land in North Africa.

1943—*January 31*: Germans surrender to the Russians at Stalingrad, marking the greatest defeat to date for the German army.

May 12: Germans retreat from North Africa.

July 10: British and American troops land in Sicily.

September 3: The British and Americans invade Italy.

1944—*June 6*: D-Day; The Allies land at Normandy.

July 25: United States forces break out of the Normandy pocket and begin a race across France.

August 26: Paris is liberated.

1945—*April 30*: Hitler commits suicide in his Berlin bunker.

May 7: Germany surrenders to the Allies.

★ CHAPTER NOTES ★

Chapter 1. The First Strike

1. Stephen E. Ambrose, *D-Day, June 6, 1944: The Climactic Battle of World War II* (New York: Touchstone Books, 1994), p. 22.

Chapter 2. Conquered Europe

1. William L. Shirer, *The Rise and Fall of the Third Reich* (New York: Simon and Schuster, 1960), p. 658.

Chapter 3. Operation Overlord

1. Richard Goldstein, *America at D-Day* (New York: Dell Publishing, 1994), p. 10.

2. Cornelius Ryan, *The Longest Day* (New York: Simon and Schuster, 1959), p. 27.

3. *Gallimard Guide Series Battle of Normandy* (Paris, France: Gallimard Guides, 1994), p. 115.

4. Jon E. Lewis, ed., *Eye-Witness D-Day* (New York: Carroll & Graf Publishers, Inc, 1994), p. 15.

5. Dwight D. Eisenhower, *Crusade in Europe* (New York: Doubleday & Company, Inc., 1948), p. 251.

6. Stephen E. Ambrose, *D-Day, June 6, 1944: The Climactic Battle of World War II* (New York: Touchstone Books, 1994), p. 45.

7. Lewis, p. 36.

8. Ambrose, p. 187.

9. Lewis, p. 52.

Chapter 4. Assault From the Air

1. Jon E. Lewis, ed., *Eye-Witness D-Day* (New York: Carroll & Graf Publishers, Inc, 1994), p. 81.

2. Douglas Botting, *The Second Front* (Alexandria, Virginia: Time-Life Books, 1978), p. 137.

3. Stephen E. Ambrose, *D-Day, June 6, 1944: The Climactic Battle of World War II* (New York: Touchstone Books, 1994), p. 201.

4. Cornelius Ryan, *The Longest Day* (New York: Simon and Schuster, 1959), p. 131.

5. Lewis, p. 82.

6. Ibid.

7. Richard Goldstein, *America at D-Day* (New York: Dell Publishing, 1994), p. 70.

8. Ambrose, p. 206.

9. Ryan, p. 139.

10. Lewis, p. 85.

11. Ambrose, p. 317.

12. Botting, pp. 101–102.

Chapter 5. Assault From the Sea

1. Stephen E. Ambrose, *D-Day, June 6, 1944: The Climactic Battle of World War II* (New York: Touchstone Books, 1994), p. 244.

2. Richard Goldstein, *America at D-Day* (New York: Dell Publishing, 1994), p. 75.

3. David Nichols, ed., *Ernie's War: The Best of Ernie Pyle's World War II Dispatches* (New York: Random House, 1986), p. 276.

4. Ambrose, p. 263.

5. Cornelius Ryan, *The Longest Day* (New York: Simon and Schuster, 1959), p. 200.

6. Ronald J. Drez, ed., *Voices of D-Day* (Baton Rouge: Louisiana State University Press, 1994), p. 170.

7. Ibid.

8. Ibid., p. 173.

9. Gerald Astor, *June 6, 1944: The Voices of D-Day* (New York: Random House, 1994), p. 277.

10. Ryan, p. 231.

11. Ibid., p. 232.

12. Ibid., p. 233.

13. Ambrose, p. 282.

14. Jon E. Lewis, ed., *Eye-Witness D-Day* (New York: Carroll & Graf Publishers, Inc, 1994), p. 152.

15. Douglas Botting, *The Second Front* (Alexandria, Virginia: Time-Life Books, 1978), p. 132.

16. Ambrose, p. 401.

17. Ibid., p. 399.

18. Botting, p. 139.

19. Astor, p. 306.

20. Ibid., p. 307.

21. Ambrose, p. 541.

Chapter 6. Bloody Omaha

1. Douglas Botting, *The Second Front* (Alexandria, Virginia: Time-Life Books, 1978), p. 137.

2. Stephen E. Ambrose, *D-Day, June 6, 1944: The Climactic Battle of World War II* (New York: Touchstone Books, 1994), p. 343.

3. Cornelius Ryan, *The Longest Day* (New York: Simon and Schuster, 1959), p. 228.

4. Ambrose, p. 331.

5. Gerald Astor, *June 6, 1944: The Voices of D-Day* (New York: Random House, 1994), p. 227.

6. Jon E. Lewis, ed., *Eye-Witness D-Day* (New York: Carroll & Graf Publishers, Inc, 1994), p. 103.

7. Ambrose, p. 356.

8. Ibid., p. 359.

9. Botting, p. 140.

10. Ambrose, pp. 386–387.

11. Ibid., p. 388.

12. Ibid., pp. 392–393.

13. Ibid., p. 396.

14. Lewis, p. 106.

15. Ambrose, p. 357.

16. Ibid., p. 447.

17. Ibid., p. 454.

Chapter 7. The Battle of Normandy

1. Jon E. Lewis, ed., *Eye-Witness D-Day* (New York: Carroll & Graf Publishers, Inc, 1994), p. 231.

2. Cornelius Ryan, *The Longest Day* (New York: Simon and Schuster, 1959), p. 285.

3. Ibid., p. 285.

4. Lewis, p. 92.

5. Stephen E. Ambrose, *D-Day, June 6, 1944: The Climactic Battle of World War II* (New York: Touchstone Books, 1994), p. 481.

6. Richard Goldstein, *America at D-Day* (New York: Dell Publishing, 1994), p. 110.

7. Ibid., p. 113.

8. Ibid., p. 262.

9. Gerald Astor, *June 6, 1944: The Voices of D-Day* (New York: Random House, 1994), p. 361.

10. Dwight D. Eisenhower, *Crusade in Europe* (New York: Doubleday & Company, Inc., 1948), p. 269.

Chapter 8. The Aftermath

1. Stephen E. Ambrose, *D-Day, June 6, 1944: The Climactic Battle of World War II* (New York: Touchstone Books, 1994), p. 469.

2. William L. Shirer, *The Rise and Fall of the Third Reich* (New York: Simon and Schuster, 1960), p. 1039.

3. Ibid.

4. Ambrose, p. 583.

★ FURTHER READING ★

Black, Wallace B., and Jean F. Blashfield. *D-Day*. New York: Macmillan, 1992.

Devaney, John. *America Storms the Beaches, 1944*. New York: Walker and Company, 1993.

Green, Robert. *Vive La France: The French Resistance During World War II*. Danbury, Conn.: Franklin Watts, 1995.

Pietrusza, David. *The Invasion of Normandy: Battles of World War II*. Farmington Hills, Mich.: Gale Group, 1996.

Sinnot, Susan. *Doing Our Part: American Women on the Home Front in World War II*. Danbury, Conn.: Franklin Watts, 1995.

Stewart, Gail B. *Hitler's Reich*. San Diego: Lucent Books, 1994.

Whitman, Sylvia. *V is for Victory: The American Home Front in World War II*. Minneapolis: Lerner Books, 1993.

★ INTERNET ADDRESSES ★

"D-Day." *American Experience*. n.d. <http://www.pbs.org/wgbh/amex/dday>.

The National D-Day Memorial Foundation. n.d. <http://www.dday.org>.

The National D-Day Museum. © 2003. <http://www.ddaymuseum.org>.

★ INDEX ★